Voices from the Field

Learning from the

Early Work

of Comprehensive

Community Initiatives

ROUNDTABLE ON
COMPREHENSIVE
COMMUNITY
INITIATIVES FOR
CHILDREN AND
FAMILIES

THE
ASPEN INSTITUTE

HN
90
.C6
V65
1997

The Aspen Institute
Suite 1070
1333 New Hampshire Avenue, NW
Washington, DC 20036

Published in the United States of America in 1997 by The Aspen Institute

Printed in the United States of America

ISBN #0-89843-228-6

Contents

Acknowledgements

The Roundtable on Comprehensive Community Initiatives for Children and Families was established in 1992 as a forum in which people engaged in the field of comprehensive community initiatives (CCIs)—including foundation sponsors, directors, technical assistance providers, evaluators, and public sector officials—could meet to discuss the lessons that are being learned by initiatives across the country and to work on common problems that they are facing. (A list of Roundtable members is included as appendix A.) In addition to the project that has resulted in this report, the Roundtable is examining a range of specific issues that are critical to the CCI field. For example, to address the challenges associated with evaluating CCIs, the Roundtable regularly convenes a Steering Committee on Evaluation. The first phase of that committee's work is presented in *New Approaches to Evaluating Community Initiatives: Concepts, Methods, and Contexts*, edited by James P. Connell, Anne C. Kubisch, Lisbeth B. Schorr, and Carol H. Weiss, published by the Aspen Institute in 1995. A second volume on CCI evaluation is scheduled for publication during 1998.

In 1995, members of the Roundtable pointed to the need to systematically distill the experiences of the current generation of CCIs in order to: (a) inform work on important cross-cutting issues that are at the forefront of the CCI field, such as comprehensiveness of program, community building, and related operational challenges; (b) suggest next steps to enhance the effectiveness of currently operating CCIs; (c) guide new program architects and implementers; and (d) define a research agenda for further learning and application.

The co-chairs and staff of the Roundtable responded to this charge by designing a participatory process with the aim of eliciting the observations of fellow actors in the CCI field and producing an analytical portrait of CCIs that could be of use to a number of audiences. Over the course of a two-month period, June - July 1995, the Roundtable sponsored eleven focus group discussions, each with 6-14 "peers" in the CCI field—defined as people occupying similar positions, including foundation representatives, initiative directors and staff, evaluators, members of the governance structures of local initiatives, residents of the neighborhoods in which CCIs are taking place, and other experts and observers of the field. By the end of the process, 94 individuals participated in the day-long structured discussion sessions, which were taped, transcribed, and analyzed for presentation in this report. (Further discussion of the methodology that was used and a list of the participants in the focus group sessions can be found in appendices B and C.)

In the series of peer group discussions that informed this report, participants were asked to consider their experiences and the lessons they are learning about CCI goals, principles, operational strategies, and programs. In analyzing the data, however, it became apparent that a simple reporting of the observations of actors within these static categories would understate the complexity of the CCI phenomenon and would do a disservice to the depth of knowledge that is being generated through CCIs about how to promote significant and lasting change in poor neighborhoods. It is the dynamics of CCIs that are important to understand—that is, the interplay among goals, principles, operations, and programs. This report, therefore, emphasizes and explores what is being learned about those dynamics.

Although seven people were responsible for putting pen to paper and serving as the scribes for this project, in many ways it was the 94 people who participated in our focus group sessions who "wrote" this report. Please refer to Appendix B for this list of the focus group participants, the true authors of this report.

The activities that led to the production of this paper were led by Anne C. Kubisch, director of the Roundtable. She was joined by six people, and the team worked together throughout all stages of the project: defining the scope of work, conducting the focus group sessions, analyzing the data, identifying the key messages that the data suggested, and writing the report. Three of the team members were Roundtable staff, three were staff of the Chapin Hall Center for

Children at the University of Chicago, and one belonged to both institutions:

- Anne C. Kubisch, Roundtable Director
- Prudence Brown, Associate Director, Chapin Hall
- Robert Chaskin, Research Fellow, Chapin Hall
- Janice Hirota, Roundtable Consultant
- Mark Joseph, Research Associate, Chapin Hall
- Harold Richman, Roundtable Co-Chair, and Director, Chapin Hall
- Michelle Roberts, Roundtable Program Associate

The Roundtable's activities are funded by ten foundations and two federal departments: the Ford Foundation, the Robert Wood Johnson Foundation, the Pew Charitable Trusts, the Foundation for Child Development, the Annie E. Casey Foundation, the C. S. Mott Foundation, the Edna McConnell Clark Foundation, the W. K. Kellogg Foundation, the John D. and Catherine T. MacArthur Foundation, the Spencer Foundation, the U.S. Department of Housing and Urban Development, and the U.S. Department of Health and Human Services. The co-chairs and staff of the Roundtable are grateful to their foundation and government sponsors, who made this work possible. The Roundtable is also grateful to the Chapin Hall Center for Children at the University of Chicago for lending its staff to this project and to the Foundation for Child Development, which provided office space and other generous support for the Roundtable's work.

Many people assisted in this effort and provided important feedback on earlier drafts. On behalf of the authors, we thank them all. Several people deserve special mention: Barbara Blum, Sid Gardner, Craig Howard, Sarah Ingersoll, Rebecca Riley, and Rebecca Stone. In addition, thanks go to all the members of the Roundtable who helped us to frame both the project and the final product. Two Chapin Hall staff deserve special thanks: Susan Campbell for her expert editing and Sylvan Robb for her work on the initiative descriptions that informed our work. Finally, many thanks go to Anne Mackinnon, Rick Landesberg, Carolyn Uhl, and Sylvia Pear for producing this final version of the report.

The authors are solely responsible for the accuracy of the statements and the interpretations contained within this report. The interpretations do not necessarily reflect the views of the sponsoring foundations or of the federal government.

Finally, and most important of all, we thank the 94 people who participated in the peer group discussions and shared their experiences and wisdom with us. As suggested by its title, *Voices from the Field*, the aim of this report is to explore and capture the wisdom of those who are actively engaged in CCIs today. We hope that they find their "voices" represented here.

Harold Richman, Roundtable Co-Chair
    Hermon Dunlap Smith Professor of Social Welfare Policy
    Director, Chapin Hall Center for Children
    University of Chicago

Lisbeth B. Schorr, Roundtable Co-Chair
    Director, Harvard Project on Effective Interventions
    Harvard University

Terms and Quotations

In the discussion that follows, we use a number of terms that are widely employed in the field, but often with a variety of meanings. For the sake of clarity, we offer the following definitions:

Participants: Individuals who are *directly* involved in the implementation of a given initiative, including members of the governance structure, staff, and neighborhood residents, but *not* including funders, evaluators, technical assistance providers, and consultants

Initiative: A local, single-site CCI (or the local manifestation of a multi-site CCI)

Neighborhood: A geographically defined portion of a larger municipality that constitutes the target area of a CCI

Community: Individuals and organizations in the neighborhood linked through networks of affective and instrumental connections

Community building: The process of improving the quality of life in a neighborhood by strengthening the capacity of neighborhood residents, associations, and organizations to identify priorities and opportunities and to work, individually and collectively, to foster and sustain positive neighborhood change

Neighborhood change: The goal sought by CCIs, including increased capacity, access to opportunity, and quality of life of individuals and families; improvement of the existence, accessibility, and quality of facilities, services, opportunities, and circumstances within the neighborhood; and increased quantity and quality of services, facilities, investments, and opportunities provided by systems beyond the neighborhood

Funder: The initiative's sponsor or convenor; the term "funder" was chosen because it is widely used and highlights the critical influence of money in initiative relationships

Stakeholders: Individuals and organizations defined by an initiative as having a direct interest in the well-being of the neighborhood

Systems: The institutions and structural influences beyond the neighborhood that define the broader environment of which the neighborhood and initiative are a part, such as the government (at the municipal, county, state, and national levels), the structure of services, and the economy (local, regional, and national)

A note on the use of quotations. The learning presented in this report is synthesized from the experiences, perceptions, and convictions of a broad range of CCI participants and other stakeholders in the field. Direct quotes are used frequently and should be understood as illustrative of the general sentiment regarding an issue, unless otherwise noted. We identify the peer group from which a respondent speaks only in cases where that information is particularly relevant to understanding its implications.

Introduction

Comprehensive community initiatives (CCIs) are neighborhood-based efforts that seek to improve the lives of individuals and families, as well as the conditions of the neighborhoods in which they reside. This report presents a framework for understanding the challenges and potential of the approach taken by CCIs to neighborhood revitalization. It defines the goals, principles, operations, and program activities of CCIs, with an emphasis on how they interact and inform one another. Most of the lessons that can be drawn about the field at this point are best understood with reference to those dynamics and the tensions that they create as a CCI is implemented.

The CCI Phenemenon and Its Implications

This report emphasizes that the growing field of CCIs is defined as much by *how* the initiatives work to promote individual and neighborhood well-being, and by *who* makes the decisions and does the work, as by *what* actually gets done. The implication of this finding for general social policy and for the design of poverty alleviation programs is significant. It implies that neighborhood transformation may depend less on putting into place a model configuration of comprehensive neighborhood-based activities than on developing capacity at the neighborhood level to define and effect responses to local needs on a sustained basis. This is not to suggest that more and better programs, increased economic activity and opportunities, and improvements in housing and neighborhood conditions are unimportant. Rather, it warns that these alone they will be insufficient to achieve the kind of change that is needed in distressed neighborhoods today and into the future. It also suggests that unless local capacity is strong, program elements such as services, housing, and crime reduction will achieve only a fraction of their potential.

At the same time, however, the "tools" that are available for the majority of community change efforts across the country have been cast in the "old" mold of discrete program activities. To a large extent, foundations still operate as grantmakers rather than partners in the change process; funding is still allocated in short-term intervals; technical assistance is still provided on a problem-specific, temporary basis; evaluation is still focused on measuring broad indicators that can be unambiguously linked to particular interventions; and capacity building and community building are still considered secondary to putting programs on the ground. CCIs represent the field's best attempt to modify and apply those rusty tools to current neighborhood circumstances—and, in some CCIs, new tools are even being forged—but because those tools are not well suited to the task at hand, funda-mental tensions emerge as CCIs attempt to put their guiding principles into practice.

These findings also suggest that fundamental and lasting neigh-borhood change will require all actors to move beyond traditional definitions of their roles. Initiative staff, governance participants, funders, technical assistance providers, and evaluators will be required to take on multiple and overlapping roles, and the definition of "stakeholders" in the neighborhood will need to be broadened. Moreover, the complexity of the CCI undertaking requires a rethinking of how these players interact with one another and, in the words of one CCI stakeholder, the development of "new partnerships for change" at the neighborhood level.

Understanding the Complex Dynamics of CCIs

CCIs are based on two principles: comprehensiveness and community building. In the interest of comprehensiveness, CCIs work across social, economic, and physical sectors and attempt to foster synergy among them. Toward community building, CCIs work to strengthen the capacity of individuals, associations, and institutions in the neighbor-hood to enhance community well-being. Translating these principles into action is what makes CCIs so complex and challenging.

The principles of comprehensiveness and community building are enacted through a variety of strategies—including governance, funding, staffing, technical assistance, and evaluation—which in turn spearhead or support the development and implementation of particular programmatic activities. How the initiative actually unfolds will be the result of how the involved actors—including funders, directors and staff, residents and other stakeholders—define and enact the goals, principles and other component parts of the model. Thus, while the core principles are shared, individual participant perspectives about the operationalization of the principles often differ greatly, and may sometimes be in opposition, creating tensions within the initiatives. In this analysis of the CCI phenomenon, two central tensions are introduced and examined in depth: the tension between "process" and "product" and the tension between "inside" and "outside."

The process-product tension, emerging out of the need to attend to both means and ends on a continuous basis, is a central by-product of the community building agenda. At one level, CCIs are process-driven. They seek to catalyze and support the creation of mechanisms to sustain a process of decision making, capacity building, and implementation rooted in the circumstances of neighborhood residents and other "stakeholders." At the same time, CCIs seek to promote broad and measurable changes in the quality of life of neighborhoods and their residents. A balance needs to be struck between these two objectives, and where aims are competing they need to be negotiated.

The inside-outside tension is fundamentally about relationships. This tension is defined by the fact that CCIs are construed as locally driven, locally controlled efforts at neighborhood transformation, while at the same time they are catalyzed, supported, guided, monitored, and studied by actors and institutions beyond the neighborhood. It is also fundamentally about power and authority—about who makes what decisions, when, and how. The relationship between the funder of a CCI, and often by extension the technical assistance provider and evaluator, and the neighborhood in which it seeks to support change is paradigmatic of the inside-outside tension. It is not, however, the only relationship that exemplifies it. In CCIs, there are many insides and many outsides, and the boundaries that define them often shift according to shifting circumstances and perspectives. In the operation of CCIs any of a number of participants may at one point or another be seen by some as "outside" to their "inside." The tension is thus not just about power, but about legitimacy, accountability, representation, and respect.

These two tensions are inherent in the nature of CCIs. They may be creative or debilitating. When they are successfully negotiated by the participants in an ongoing give-and-take, they may support a dialectical process in which interaction between poles—process and product, or inside and outside—enriches planning and implementation and guides the CCI toward its long-term goals.

The Scope of This Report

The report begins in chapter 1 by introducing and describing the CCI phenomenon: the goals of individual, neighborhood, and system change; the core principles of comprehensiveness and community building; the operational dimensions of governance, funding, staffing, technical assistance, and evaluation; and the programs that CCIs undertake covering the social, economic, physical aspects of individual and neighborhood well-being.

Chapter 2 focuses on two central tensions that appear to be intrinsic to a CCI. They are the tension between "process" and "product" and the tension between "inside" and "outside." Many of the operational lessons to be learned from CCIs at this point can be understood in terms of, or as reflections of, the two tensions. They underlie intent, interaction, and interpretation. They can be seen in the relationships among stakeholders, in the processes of strategic planning and project implementation, and in the monitoring of progress toward particular objectives. While there are discrete, practical lessons to be learned from the experience of CCIs, to focus solely on these lessons without first exploring the fundamental dynamics that affect them is, in the view of the authors of this report, insufficient for understanding the nature of CCIs and of limited value in applying the lessons to practice.

Drawing on the elements described in chapter 1, chapter 3 then summarizes early findings. It is important to remember that any "lessons" that emerge from the analysis of the tensions in chapter 2 are derived only from the start-up phases of CCI initiatives. Operational findings are limited in part because of the relative newness of the CCI field. Even the most long-standing of the current generation of CCIs have been in place for perhaps seven or eight years, and most are much younger.

Thus, what this report cannot tell us is whether CCIs are powerful enough to deliver on their promise. The nature, scope, and scale of activities that are being undertaken may still be inadequate to transform impoverished neighborhoods: contextual circumstances beyond the influence of a neighborhood-based initiative may overwhelm local efforts, however meritorious they may be. Certainly those who have participated in this analysis, whether as funders, directors and staff, evaluators, governance members, or neighborhood residents, believe strongly in the potential of CCIs. It is for this reason that they shared so openly with us their experience and the conclusions they are drawing from their work. But there is also a sense that this is only a beginning and that much remains to be learned.

1

CCI Goals, Principles, and Operational Strategies

In recent years, funders, policy makers, and program designers have been exploring a range of approaches to revitalizing distressed neighborhoods. One important branch of these efforts is known in the field as "comprehensive community initiatives," or CCIs. They are neighborhood-based efforts that seek to improve the lives of individuals and families, as well as the conditions of the neighborhoods in which they reside, by working comprehensively across social, economic, and physical sectors. They are based upon the concept of "community building" and are structured to promote individual and community empowerment. Beginning with a handful of nascent initiatives in the late 1980s, foundation-funded CCIs now number close to fifty. Government is also increasingly involved in comparable efforts, including the federal empowerment zones and a variety of city- and state-driven initiatives. This growing number of CCIs and similar endeavors suggests that the principles that underlie CCIs will continue to guide many aspects of current and future anti-poverty activities.

The CCI movement is, in part, a reaction against recent practice in the social welfare and economic development fields and, in part, a reformulation of earlier approaches. As a reaction against past practice, CCIs seek to replace piecemeal, categorical approaches with "comprehensive" efforts that cross sectoral and programmatic boundaries and attempt to build on the interconnections among economic, social, and physical needs and opportunities. As a reformulation of earlier approaches, CCIs build on the conceptual foundations of community development theory and practice that are represented by the Gray Areas Program, the Community Action Program, the Community Development Corporation movement, and related efforts. They employ the lessons from those experiences not so much as "models" for action but as a set of basic guiding concepts—including comprehensiveness, coordination, collaboration, and community participation and empowerment—and then use a wide range of organizational and programmatic strategies to promote positive community change.

While the individual efforts that constitute the field of comprehensive community-based initiatives differ significantly in structure and in the *programs* they put into place, they hold in common a set of fundamental *goals*, they are guided by a shared set of general *principles*, and they encounter similar *operational* needs and challenges. The abstract model visualized here provides a way to sort through the tangled on-the-ground implementation and operational dynamics of CCIs.

**The Interplay
of Goals, Principles,
Operations and
Programs**

Fundamental Goals of CCIs

Comprehensive community-based initiatives are defined in part by the ambitious goals they set for themselves. These goals go well beyond the remediation of particular problems, such as teenage pregnancy or insufficient income, or the development of particular assets, such as housing stock or new social services. CCIs attempt instead to foster a fundamental transformation of poor neighborhoods and to catalyze a process of sustained improvement in the circumstances and opportunities of individuals and families in those neighborhoods. They seek, furthermore, to change the nature of the relationship between the neighborhood and the systems outside its boundaries by ensuring that change is locally grounded but also draws upon external sources of knowledge and resources. Thus, CCIs set out to promote change at three levels: the individual or family, the neighborhood, and the broader, or system-level, context.

Change at the Individual and Family Levels

CCIs seek to build capacity and improve the quality of life of individual neighborhood residents and their families. They aim to increase both the quality and quantity of activities designed to improve educational outcomes, employment, and the health and well-being of neighborhood residents. At the same time, CCIs place priority on strengthening the personal, political, or "process" skills that enable people to motivate and lead their peers. They recognize that their neighborhoods need both types of individual development, and deliberately build both into the agenda.

Neighborhood-Level Change

CCIs are concerned with the accessibility and quality of social support, economic opportunity, and physical infrastructure within the target neighborhood. This generally encompasses efforts to improve or increase the housing stock, neighborhood infrastructure, the business/commercial sector, education and training institutions, the social and civic support network, cultural vitality, and other quality-of-life activities. By and large, the strategies that CCIs pursue focus on building the capacity of existing local institutions responsible for these aspects of neighborhood life, or supporting the creation of new organizations to do so. CCIs are also concerned with the qualities of collective life provided through community attributes such as strong personal networks, "social capital," and a "sense of community," as well as the neighborhood's capacity to handle conflict, solve problems, and/or express its voice and represent its interests in the larger economic and political arena. By definition, these are qualities of neighborhoods, and the unit of analysis is the collective, not the individual.

Systems-Level Change

Change within a broader context is often necessary in order to create individual and neighborhood change that is holistic and sustainable. CCIs explicitly seek to improve the quantity and quality of services and other investments provided by outside systems (including social services, schools, the judicial system, commercial activity, and private sector investment) and to increase access for neighborhood residents to the structure of opportunity that exists at the municipal or regional level. This often involves a political empowerment agenda for the neighborhood that includes community organizing, better representation of neighborhood interests in city-level decision-making forums, or gaining commitments for improved corporate responsibility toward the neighborhood.

Central Principles of CCIs

CCIs hold in common a set of principles that guide their creation and unfolding. The two central principles, under which other basic convictions are subsumed, are *comprehensiveness* and *community building*.

Comprehensiveness

The principle of comprehensiveness addresses the full range of circumstances, opportunities, and needs of individuals and families living in CCI neighborhoods and the relationships among them. Their interrelationship argues against categorical approaches that focus on discrete problems or opportunities in isolation from other facets of life. A focus on the creation of jobs in a given neighborhood, for example, without taking into account residents' educational circumstances, or their need for supports such as child care, transportation, and training, would be limited both in vision and in potential benefits. The principle of comprehensiveness calls for constant consideration of systemic connections among issues.

Most CCIs give attention to the following goals, in principle if not yet in action, and aim to achieve synergy among them. Some of the activities that CCIs take on in pursuit of those goals are also listed:

- **Expansion and improvement of social services:** Filling service gaps in the neighborhood, co-locating and integrating social services, or promoting developmental rather than remedial social services

- **Education and training:** Encouraging school reform, organizing job training and placement programs, or developing local leadership

- **Economic development:** Working with financial institutions to ensure investment in the neighborhood, providing loan funds and technical assistance for small business development, or providing capital for neighborhood projects

- **Physical revitalization:** Collaborating with a community development corporation, public housing agency, or private-sector investors to improve housing or physical spaces

- **Quality-of-life activities:** Working with local police to improve safety, establishing community gardens, developing a recreation center, improving environmental conditions, promoting ties across diverse ethnic communities, or organizing cultural celebrations

The charge to think comprehensively is normally interpreted as working across these various sectors. CCIs aim to recognize and reinforce positive connections among them in order to enhance chances for improving outcomes.

Community Building

The principle of community building is explicitly stated in the charge of most initiatives and implicit in both the mission and approach of all CCIs. Fundamentally, community building has to do with strengthening the capacity of neighborhood residents, associations, and organizations to work, individually and collectively, to foster and sustain positive neighborhood change. For individuals, community building focuses on enhancing the capacity of neighborhood residents to access resources and effect change in their lives through a range of mechanisms, with leadership development often playing a central role. At the associational level, community building focuses on the nature, strength, and scope of relationships (both affective and instrumental) among individuals within the neighborhood and, through them, connections to networks of association beyond the neighborhood. These are ties of kinship, acquaintance, or other more formal means through which information, resources, and assistance can be delivered. Finally, for organizations, community building centers on developing the capacity of formal and informal institutions within the neighborhood to provide goods and services effectively, and on the relationships among organizations both within and beyond the neighborhood to maximize resources and coordinate strategies for neighborhood improvement.

CCIs aim to be effective vehicles for building capacity among residents, among neighborhood associations or networks, and among formal neighborhood institutions. They view residents and local institutions as *agents of change* rather than as beneficiaries or clients. CCIs, therefore, are as much about *how* neighborhood transformation occurs as they are about putting into place a comprehensive set of programs that might produce that transformation. All CCI participants, in one way or another, emphasize that creating connections among people and among institutions is a core theme, or even *the* core theme, of their efforts.

Operational Strategies

To translate these principles into action that can foster broad neighborhood change, CCIs make strategic choices that are reflected in their structures and operations. These strategies are manifest in various aspects of CCIs, including governance, funding, staffing, technical assistance, evaluation, and program development.

Governance

In many ways, governance is the key operational dimension of CCIs and the one through which the other operating strategies are negotiated and played out. It concerns the creation of mechanisms to guide planning, decision making, and implementation, as well as to locate accountability and responsibility for action undertaken.

Because the change strategies represented by CCIs are formulated as *initiatives* that seek to engage in comprehensive action, the functions of governance—participation, planning, decision making, oversight, program implementation—tend to be formalized. This may take shape in a nonprofit entity newly created for the purpose of initiative governance. Alternatively, the governance function may be assumed by a collaboration among individuals or among institutions, usually but not always allied with an established organization such as a community foundation or a community development corporation. Almost invariably, however, these initiative governance structures are designed to include in their membership a diverse body of "stakeholders," including neighborhood residents, local business owners and civic leaders, representatives of various community-based organizations, members of public-sector agencies including city government officials, and members of the private and nonprofit sectors in the broader community. Often in a single initiative, there are several layers of governance that structure the roles of local and non-local participants, including funders, staff, technical assistance providers and consultants, and evaluators.

Governance is thus both structure and process: it attempts to operationalize the central principles of comprehensiveness and community building through the organized engagement of a range of participants both within and beyond the target neighborhood. Comprehensiveness is addressed by assembling participants with different experiences, different fields of expertise, and different access to resources who, through interaction and common endeavor, might overcome categorical boundaries. Similarly, the very process of community building is accomplished, in part, as a result of initiative governance because a variety of "stakeholders"—from neighborhood residents to city leaders—become engaged in neighborhood transformation in a formalized way.

Funding

CCIs are generally foundation-sponsored initiatives. Grant funds are meant to be flexible and responsive to the priorities established by the local governance structure. Generally, however, CCI funds are not used to cover ongoing program costs, but are used instead for planning and management, capacity building, seed funding for new activities, and the like. CCI funds are not meant to replace major public-sector funding streams such as education or safety or private-sector investment, but rather to help ensure that those dollars are used as effectively as possible and to leverage increased financial flows into the neighborhood.

Staffing

Most neighborhood initiatives rely to a large extent on a core staff person who, as project director or coordinator, facilitates the planning process and takes responsibility for moving from planning to action. In some CCIs, additional staff provide administrative assistance or manage individual activities, such as community organizing or specific CCI projects. As the complement of staff in an initiative grows, CCIs generally place high priority on recruiting from the neighborhood itself.

The staff may be located in a "neutral" organization, such as a local intermediary or a community foundation, in a newly created organization or collaborative structure, or in a specially created slot within an existing neighborhood entity such as a community development corporation. Regardless of where staff members are based, they are generally accountable to the wide range of CCI stakeholders.

Technical Assistance

The provision of technical assistance in CCIs takes several forms and is meant to serve several functions. Technical assistance may be provided centrally by a funder or it may be sought by the CCI governance entity and other participants. It may be furnished by one or multiple providers. It may focus on process issues (such as governance, board development, strategic planning) or programmatic issues (such as service provision, land use, financial instruments). Technical assistance providers may be used as supplementary staff to get concrete work done or they may be asked to promote long-term capacity building by focusing on the transference of skills and knowledge to neighborhood residents or organizations. Each of these choices may support or complicate adherence to the principles that guide CCIs, and may have a significant impact on the structure, processes, and outcomes of a given initiative.

Evaluation

Evaluation in CCIs generally serves at least four functions, any one of which might be more or less emphasized depending on the particular initiative, its developmental stage, and its funder. First, evaluation can be formative, providing feedback to various initiative stakeholders, such as funders, staff, or residents. Because CCIs are generally recognized to be learning enterprises, formative evaluation is often given high priority. Second, evaluation might be more summative, seeking to provide evidence of ultimate or periodic progress after a given period of time. Third, CCI evaluation might serve a "social learning" function, attempting to draw out generalizable lessons for policy and for future research and experimentation. Finally, CCI evaluation can promote the community capacity building and empowerment agenda of an initiative, especially if evaluation tools such as theory specification, data collection, and information analysis are in the hands of the residents or community institutions.

Evaluation may be provided—or imposed—by funders or sought out by local participants; it may work with or separately from other institutional support components such as staff, technical assistance, and funding; it may engage participants to varying degrees in design, implementation, and analysis. As with technical assistance, these choices relate differently to the principles that guide CCIs, and they may affect both ongoing implementation of and ultimate learning from a given initiative.

Program Development

Given the broad goals of CCIs and the broadly stated principles of comprehensiveness and community building, the scope, direction, and intent of programs developed under the initiatives are virtually unconstrained. They often cover a wide range of functional areas and seek a wide range of outcomes. The set of programmatic choices made by a CCI less often constitute a coherent approach in themselves than an effort to enhance, build on, and support programmatic activity already in existence. Thus, programmatically, CCIs seek to fill gaps, connect resources and activities, build capacity, and organize constituent elements of the communities in which they work.

2

Dynamic Tensions
in Early CCI Practice

Ambitious in their goals and complex in structure, CCIs tend to give rise to two types of tension—between product and process and between inside and outside—during the early phases of their work.

The Product-Process Tension

CCIs are by nature long-term enterprises. Even if they eventually succeed, it will take years, if not decades, to achieve the magnitude of improvement to which these initiatives aspire. Moreover, creating the conditions for sustaining such change over time requires investment in the capacity of individuals and institutions in the neighborhood, and the returns on this kind of investment are often not seen for years. But at the same time, CCI stakeholders feel a sense of urgency about the need to change conditions for neighborhood residents and want to see progress as soon as possible. In addition, as many of the participants across the discussion groups made clear, CCIs must have something to show at a relatively early stage in order to gain and sustain support both from outside and inside the neighborhood. Funders of an initiative, for example, generally want early signs that their support is paying off and should be continued. And, neighborhood residents also need evidence that their investment—in time, energy, institutional resources, or political support—is worthwhile.

These dual realities lead to a tension between process and product in the initiatives. The tension can best be understood by defining it from each perspective. On the one hand is the difficulty of maintaining a commitment to community building, capacity building, empowerment, participation, and similar process priorities in the face of internal drives and external pressures toward products, such as better housing, more services, and new business development. On the other hand is the difficulty of achieving desired products or outcomes when process objectives, which are often time and resource consuming, are accorded such priority in the initiatives.

Searching for Balance on the Process-Product Continuum

The signs of early progress in most community revitalization efforts are generally in the form of product: housing units under construction, new street lights, or an immunization campaign. Products of this sort—that is, concrete manifestations of neighborhood improvement—are of primary importance to CCIs as well:

> **You have to have measurable successes. And you have to have them for two reasons. One, because people in the community have to see it to stay with the program, and two, you have to have it for your funding. Funders don't want to know that you went to ten meetings. They want to know, "What was measurable and what did you accomplish with this money?"**

Those who have been active in community development corporations, for example, in reviewing the history of the movement, stress the importance of their visible accomplishments. "We built buildings. We delivered. We made buildings. People saw, and that got us our legitimacy." For some, even new services are not an adequate early outcome since they are not literally "concrete" and do not produce "anything very visible to show" to the community. Those who advocate strongly for early products warn that focusing on the process of change can become all-consuming and risks not leading to any meaningful improvement in the neighborhood. As one observer suggested:

> **I've seen so many of these programs that are all process and nothing gets produced. And we can't make it that way in these poor communities …because it can look very pretty on paper and if it doesn't produce real results in those communities, why bother?**

Yet, according to others, there is a danger that, in pushing too hard for early products, an initiative sacrifices the community building potential of a neighborhood activity. In the press to get the job done, it becomes tempting to value speed and efficiency over the process of developing capacity within the neighborhood to address both today's and tomorrow's needs. Many individuals involved with a CCI can relate a story of how slippery the slope can be, as in this evaluator's description of an initiative's quick retreat to product:

> What happens, even if the organization starts out saying "We want to
> build capacity," is that it's so tempting for them to take on programs and
> operate them themselves because they'll get credit for it, because they'll
> show something concrete, which they won't if they're capacity building.
> And then the evaluators reinforce it because they say "What have you
> done?" And it's very hard to say "Well, this leadership has developed, and
> this organization is now better positioned to do different kinds of work."
> … For example, [I know of a] specific case where they started in the
> human services area with the notion of building capacity in other
> organizations to deliver family support. And what do they end up doing?
> Running their own family support center. And I see that over and over
> again, this temptation to just take over and do it [because of] credit,
> control and you can get funding for it.

Thus, a core lesson that emerges from the experience of current
CCIs is that both process and product are critical, that one without the
other will not achieve the desired goals at the individual/family,
neighborhood, and system levels. Attempting to balance the two to
achieve initiative goals, however, is no easy task and creates a
fundamental tension. If an initiative's only goals were to produce
houses, deliver services, or create jobs, this tension would hardly exist.
Likewise, it would also be less prominent if, conversely, the initiative
aimed only to strengthen social networks or enhance a participatory
development process. But a distinguishing feature of CCIs is that, in
addition to seeking improvements in the lives of individuals and in
neighborhoods, they also place value on the process of change and, in
particular, on ensuring that capacity building occurs at the same time
as program activities. According to one person:

> The CCI strategy is making sure that every objective stands for two
> things: an end in and of itself, and a stage of development, a means to a
> later end, whatever that end might be.… If houses are built, fine. But the
> fact that houses are built is a demonstration of your capacity. And that's
> its importance. It's not about building houses. Because we could have
> funded you to build houses [in a much less complicated way]. That's not
> what it was about. It was your ability to understand that you needed
> houses, your ability to internalize it sufficiently, to access the resources
> that you needed, to learn how to access resources, bring those resources
> in and build your houses as a step towards something else.

Stakeholders must negotiate continuously between the two objectives in order to maximize the positive and creative dimensions of the

tension, and to counter the perceived tradeoffs between process and product that push CCIs into one camp or the other. Even within a single initiative, there is often disagreement regarding the relative weight that should be placed on process and on product. At one end of the continuum are those who value the process of community building over all other activities. The continuum then moves through those who see attention to process as *critical* to CCI success to those who see it as just one of several important ingredients. The other end of the continuum is made up of those who value product first and foremost. Comments from four individuals exemplify these four points along the continuum:

- *On the process end:*

   For me housing without social capital is an empty shell which will soon crumble. Whereas social capital without houses is much more desirable because I believe that out of social capital, in the long term, there will be outcomes.

- *Process is critical, where the creation of dense social networks and the building of capacity needs to be pursued explicitly and continuously:*

   By way of metaphor, if you imagine multiple strands of DNA coming together where there is engagement and then success, and then you've got that happening with lots of different people around lots of different issues—all of those things together are social capital.... The CDC people may be coming together around housing issues; the arts and education people are coming together around after-school programs and school reform using arts as a tool of curricular integration; the economic development folks, sometimes drawing from these other people, are coming together about potential commercial development. In each of those things there's a product... or a purpose for the coming together, which then encourages people to come together again for other purposes.

- *Process is important, especially as a vehicle for enhancing outcomes:*

   There's a lot of opportunity for capacity building within the actual process of doing.... The rent-up process [an effort to get residents to move into new housing] is a terrific example of how we did the wrong thing. We hired a bunch of people, piece workers, you know, paid them per interview, boom-boom-boom-boom. They interviewed all these people, they did the site visit, the home visit, they got the people in, they filled up these buildings with people. They were all tax credit eligible.

> **Then our piece workers left and suddenly we had all these buildings and we didn't know who any of these people were who were living in them and they didn't know each other. The next round, what we did was we got our first group of ten people. We interviewed them. We certified them, and then it was hard, we didn't meet the deadline, but we trained them to interview the other people. So essentially they selected their neighbors … and in that case we had built community, we hadn't just rented up a building.**

• *On the product end:*

> **What is it that led to the creation of the Bedford-Stuyvesant Restoration Corporation? It was Bobby Kennedy hearing, when he walked the streets, "We want to see something." They wanted to see something three dimensional. They wanted to see housing and a movie theater and so on.... It had to start with an agenda that produced something in short order.**

A large, well-funded initiative with multiple program strategies can often accommodate such differences on the process-product continuum for quite a while. But they must ultimately be reconciled at two points: when funding limitations necessitate initiative-wide agreement on programmatic priorities, and when markers of progress must be developed for evaluation and accountability purposes. For example, as one CCI director noted, in his community the senior citizens wanted to focus attention on "rebuilding" their community, strengthening relationships and recreating the safe and supportive environment that they knew as they were growing up. The young adults in that community were more interested in jobs—because of their different life cycle needs, and perhaps because they had never experienced "community" in the way remembered by their elderly neighbors—and they thought that job creation should be the CCI's focus. These two positions came into conflict when program development priorities were debated and funding decisions needed to be made. The second potential point of conflict is evaluation. As one evaluator puts it: "Funders say, 'Tell me all about community building. And, oh by the way, I'd like to see 80 units in production.'" Where should the evaluation emphasis be? Which markers of progress are important?

Being clear about the position of an initiative or individual on the process-product continuum does not mean being static. Stakeholders report that their perspectives on the relative weights of the two dimensions can change over the course of an initiative. New developments in the neighborhood or feedback about how certain strategies are working may lead to a need for mid-course correction in one direction or the other. For example, it is possible that, after several unsuccessful efforts at engaging residents, an initiative may need to pursue a different strategy for a short while. As one director describes:

> **Two things were happening. Number one, we were not meeting whatever the expectations were for resident participation on the committee level and at community meetings. And number two, we just knew very clearly that good input could come from a number of places.... So we decided to just kick off some stuff and go ahead with what we were hearing from the few residents who were involved.**

The Process-Product Tension in CCI Operations

The tension between process and product plays out throughout the course of an initiative in four important arenas. One is in the structure of the initiative itself as expressed in its governing mechanism. Second is the way in which the initiative is staffed and assisted technically. The third is in the activities that the CCI undertakes and supports, including those aimed directly at improving individual and neighborhood outcomes as well as those aimed at community building and capacity building objectives. The fourth is in the definition of success of the initiative and in the evaluation enterprise itself. In all these arenas, CCI stakeholders at all levels are gaining experience in recognizing and negotiating around the tension and have conclusions and lessons to share.

Governance: Efficiency vs. participation. A critical set of decisions faced by the funders, designers, and early participants in a CCI revolves around the overall governance mechanism for the initiative, that is: how to structure the relationships among the institutions and individuals expected to take on leadership, management, and technical roles. Not surprisingly, the various decisions that need to be made are complex, and each has a series of real and perceived tradeoffs associated with it.

The most commonly cited tradeoff is that between "building capacity" and "getting things done," or process and product. The general line of the "product" argument is that improving individual and neighborhood well-being is hard enough in poor communities without the messiness of creating new agency collaboratives, developing new leadership, developing local capacity for staffing and providing technical assistance, and inserting a community building agenda into everything from the initiative's mission to its evaluation. Why put extra burdens on the initiative? The "process" counter-argument is that any new initiative, almost by definition, is going to be time-limited. In order to sustain the positive effects of today's work over time, the neighborhood must have developed the capacity to continue to carry out good work.

The key lesson that the CCIs are learning with respect to governance is that community revitalization depends on a new way of doing business at the neighborhood level, as well as between the neighborhood and outside forces. Therefore, capacity building for neighborhood-level actors is not optional for CCIs: it is necessary. And this will be true regardless of the "start-up" institutional configuration that is chosen (that is, whether a "lead" agency is designated or a new collaborative is created; see the discussion in chapter 3) and regardless of the ultimate governance structure that is adopted by a CCI. To the extent that capacity building is viewed as being in opposition to "getting things done," many of the ways in which it is needed and can be accomplished may be missed. One funder describes how this issue surfaces repeatedly in his foundation's grant making decisions. Foundations, he explains, are in the fortunate position to create opportunities for change that is "more than merely incremental," but they quickly face a different problem:

> **Neighborhood capacity…is relatively stagnant or rising at too slow a rate to respond to real opportunities. And much of the problem is that we under-attend, in significant and consistent ways, to the issue of capacity building…. So, we are always left with the unconscionable dilemma of slowing down the process until somebody can play catch up.**

Governance is one of the most powerful tools, perhaps even the most powerful tool, at the disposal of the CCI for providing for continuous and positive interaction between process and product. The governance mechanism is, first and foremost, the vehicle through which programmatic activities are undertaken, that is, the vehicle through in which "product" is accomplished. But, at the same time, it has the ability to develop new leadership, to make new connections among people and organizations, and to create new organizations if necessary. As one person explains, governance is a necessary element for accomplishing many things, "but mostly for transforming the ways people in those neighborhoods think about themselves vis-à-vis what they can do."

One CCI strategy for transforming the ways in which people perceive their own efficacy is to build mechanisms for resident participation into the governance structure. CCI participants who are also residents, as a group, have the strongest views about the need to involve residents in all aspects of decision-making and management processes if CCIs are to become legitimate actors in their neighborhoods. In describing his initiative's weak neighborhood involvement, one resident uses the metaphor of a train leaving the station with the passenger cars, meaning the residents, left behind: "And if the train doesn't stop, the people might blow up the track." They suggest that there are very few things that can be accomplished successfully in a neighborhood without resident involvement. In fact, the only activity that appears to elicit no cautions is street cleaning. Stories abound of efforts to name a park or building or to move a basketball court to a "better" location that have caused enormous outcry. If there are things that can be done in more than one way, or if the aim is to put into place something for the benefit of the community, consultation, at a minimum, is required. And, although there are many things to do that do not appear to require consultation with community members, it's as if "they're sleeping. And if you do the wrong thing, you could find out very quickly that they weren't sleeping, they were just sitting there waiting."

There is little disagreement, however, that putting into place a participatory, representative, and empowered governance structure is not the quickest way to deliver product, at least in the short term:

> **If you wanted a comprehensive, quick array of programs whose purpose was to move synergistically and in an integrated fashion as quickly as possible in a community, I think you could make a good case that the best way to do that would be to get the seven or eight most powerful people in the city into the room and find a way for them to cut a deal with each other.**

But this perceived tradeoff between getting things done and building capacity appears to be far more pronounced in the start-up phase of an initiative than once it is underway. Indeed, once a CCI is in place, most stakeholders agree that a participatory governance structure strengthens the initiative and is the key to sustainability. There are many examples of how backlash has occurred when process has been short-circuited. A resident, who is also a member of a governing board, describes:

Certain things might need to be done in a more timely manner but…that's not possible because you have to have consensus from folks in the neighborhood. You have to have them buy into projects and developments, otherwise they're just not going to work…. Like our housing situation. If I didn't get the folks in those neighborhoods involved, I could put it up, but they sure could take it down…and I'm talking about literally taking it down. I mean, as the construction people put it up in the daytime, they'd take it apart at night time.

Staffing and technical assistance: Expertise vs. facilitating others. The process-product tension plays out in decisions regarding staffing of CCIs in the following way. Should the CCI be staffed by someone with solid technical skills who is able to put together housing deals or supervise the counselors of a family support center? Or, are technical skills secondary to "process" skills that encourage a range of actors to come to the table and work together on neighborhood problems? A clear lesson from experienced CCIs is that the set of skills relating to convening, facilitating, and supporting others in their efforts to get things done is more important. There is a sense that an initiative can contract for specific technical advice and that, in fact, hiring someone with deep and narrow expertise could distort the CCI enterprise toward that person's field.

Securing technical assistance (TA) is complicated when viewed through the lens of the process-product tension. Sometimes it is easier to invest in outside consultants to get the job done than to invest in developing the capacity of staff or of local institutions to carry out the work on an ongoing basis. That strategy may sacrifice sustainability for early products. In fact, some warn that the TA provider can actually end up operating parts of the initiative which then "undoes the purpose of TA, which is to build the capacity locally. They sort of become the staff person."

Because CCIs are committed to both process and product, they generally need both kinds of TA. But there are few TA providers who can assist in both spheres: "TA for community building and TA for the 'substance' (like community policing, housing financing, and so on)— it's not the same people." The product side of the TA supply appears to be more fully developed and readily available than process-oriented assistance, and initiative directors and staff express disappointment with their experience with the latter. CCI directors, in particular, have been challenged by developing a strategy for using technical assistance well. Some describe their frustration with the amount of time that they need to invest in TA providers in order to receive anything of value back from them. Being clear that there is a community-building agenda is a first step since it helps set the stage for a better match between provider and initiative.

There appears to be an emerging consensus that the best kind of technical assistance—TA that both provides the necessary skills and builds local capacity—is in the form of "coaching." As one director describes:

> **The idea of inventing capacity in the organization as the goal of TA can't be underestimated. When we finally figured out that we didn't want someone to come and do it for us, and that we wanted a coach instead, we actually started verbalizing our requests for help as a request for coaching.... [The best source is someone who has] done the "it" before and is able to step back from it, learn some things and then, with humility, deliver some advice.**

A longtime observer of the field who is also a technical assistance provider describes how he and his colleagues have adopted a coaching approach, but he cautions that it is far more complicated than the traditional TA method of dropping into a project, sharing your expertise, accomplishing a task, and then moving on.

> **The way we try to do this is to try to create and coach and train in the local neighborhood the capacity over time to do this for themselves. So when there is a problem, we try not to go in and solve it but to point out that there's a problem and try to get the people to solve it themselves. And to my mind, that's essential to long-run sustainability for these initiatives. That the capacity exists in the community, led by community residents, to do these things effectively over time. That's the way I think about this. [But] in that sense I've never seen it really done yet. It's an elusive ideal but we're working towards it.**

Program activities: Concrete projects vs. community building. The process-product tension also plays out in decisions regarding where to invest program dollars. There are those who feel that the CCI neighborhoods are generally so needy that priority should be placed on investments that are most likely to lead to concrete outcomes such as rehabilitated housing, expanded services, new jobs, and so on. Others have embarked on particular projects that have had "community building" as their sole objective, such as community celebrations or peer discussion groups.

By and large, CCI participants recognize that neither use of program dollars will, in and of itself, accomplish a CCI's goals. The product-oriented approach sounds too much like "the old way of doing business" that alienated residents, focused on narrow objectives, and was, in the end, not sustainable. At the same time, there is a sense of disappointment in stand-alone community building and community organizing strategies. As one person puts it, "Who spends time community building in the abstract?" Or, in the words of one director:

> **I think that organizing for the purpose of organizing…has turned off our communities. We are now really, really tired of being organized by professionals who know how to get *anything* started, who know how to do the flip charts, who know how to ask the correct questions.**

CCIs appear to be developing two strategies for resolving this process-product tension as it plays out in program development and implementation decisions. One is to weave a community building agenda organically into all aspects of a CCI's programmatic work. This is accomplished by building in multiple opportunities for participation and for leadership development, commonly by setting up a large number of task forces and committees around issues of importance to the neighborhood. This allows residents to participate in CCI activities at any number of levels, on any number of issues, and for leadership skills to emerge. One initiative director, for example, uses her core staff to identify residents who chair each of the different committees in the governance structure. For example, "there's the loan committee and the loan officer staffs that committee, but it is chaired by a resident. And that has worked very, very well for us, and it really bolsters your staff" and resident capacity.

Community building activities can then be organized around problem-solving needs such as revamping the neighborhood's family resource center or selecting the residents who will participate in a training program. As one director points out:

> **I think there are a lot of leaders in our community who are not easily identified by normal methods…and it's good to set up a format that allows leaders to emerge and let them do the organizing. We found leaders, block by block…it's just amazing. We started with three people coming, and then we had six people coming, and the last meeting we had twenty. And out of that you see the leadership emerging, just by saying "Let's come together because we want to paint houses [or undertake some other activity]."**

The second way to meet both process and product objectives is to dedicate program dollars to outreach and community organizing activities. But there is a need to refashion traditional community organizing strategies to more closely match the CCI way of operating. Various stakeholders describe how organizing within CCIs cannot be dedicated to a single issue or cause. CCIs need "process" organizing that evolves over the course of the initiative, first engaging different players in a planning and "visioning" process, then designing and implementing programs, and then reaching out anew, "marketing," and redefining program activities. Organizing along those lines "keeps people moving and growing and empowers them along the way." The need is for a "coalition agent for whoever is out there who wants to work together" on issues that no single organization could handle on its own and to represent the neighborhood to the outside world.

Thus, as one director describes, there is a critical need for community organizing, but it needs to be tailored to the dual agenda of CCIs:

> **I think it's still the essential part of building a community: making sure the people in the community have some direction, have some kind of format under which they're working and have some leaders that have emerged from that community, not who've been selected or identified by some group who have a profile of what a leader's supposed to be like.... I think the people in the community can organize a block, they can organize a PTA, they can organize an effort.**

Moreover, CCI leaders must be deliberate about making resident engagement an ongoing priority. Often, the need is perceived only episodically, but in order for positive change to be sustained, it must be continuous. This means being willing to dedicate funds to outreach and organizing activities. In the words of one director, "without someone being willing to pay for this job, it's not going to happen." It also means engaging the next generation through an ongoing effort to enroll youth and young adults in organizing activities. Directors stress the long term pay-offs of focusing young people on community needs and their potential contribution to community well-being.

> **The longer this project goes on, or its children go on, there will probably always be points in time where the people who are doing the governing will say "we need to do more community organizing." So from our point of view, it's been very essential, and an ongoing essential, but it hasn't been steady throughout.**

Traditional organizing recognizes that information is power, and CCI participants agree that it is almost impossible to over-inform the residents of the neighborhood about what the CCI is doing. Flyers, community meetings, a community newsletter, posting signs in the local stores are all essential organizing tools. Other engagement strategies include working through neighborhood institutions such as the school or the church, organizing community meetings, and developing a "block captain" system.

CCIs are also experimenting with using information in even more sophisticated ways. They are finding that neighborhood-based information and analysis can also be extremely powerful tools for resident mobilization and participation. As residents gain a better sense of the problems and strengths of their neighborhood and the dynamics that caused them, they are better positioned to determine the types of strategies that make the most sense for them. One initiative got its start though a neighbor-to-neighbor survey, where one person on each block went door to door to solicit ideas for neighborhood improvement. As the staff member describes it: "We feel that another piece of this, in terms of resident power, is we have to start putting in the hands of neighborhood people the tools, which include information, because people have to make informed decisions." A resident voices a similar perspective: "We live in the 21st century… and whoever controls the communication controls the community…. Put [communication tools] in the hands of the people and let them get the message out and communicate."

Evaluation: Counting products vs. assessing capacity. Although it is possible to launch a CCI (and even to implement it, if it is well funded) without reconciling the process-product tension, it is not possible to develop an evaluation plan for an initiative without having done so. It is, after all, in the process of designing an evaluation that specific decisions must be made regarding the type and degree of change that is sought and the measures that would indicate whether that change is occurring. For some, process indicators are more powerful than for others:

> **For our neighborhoods, the fact that the people are organized and coming together to get street lights and having the attention from downtown, for them that's progress. For our funders, it's not necessarily.**

One of the principal reasons that this tension plagues the evaluation enterprise is that all those involved with CCIs recognize that the concept of community building is hard to define and to measure. And, in any case, perhaps there is no end point of a "built" community— perhaps community building is a continually evolving process that looks different at different points in time. Because it is so difficult to define and measure these concepts, there is a temptation for CCI evaluations to downplay or miss the process dimensions of the initiative. As one evaluator reports: "That capacity building part slips off so easily, that unless [it's brought up constantly] through the training of the people you've got in the field, through the reporting system that they have, through the evaluation system,…it's so easy to ignore…."

One evaluator describes assessing community capacity in the following way:

Part of what makes it hard is that in order to know you've got it, there have to be some concrete products. You know, you did the houses or the lot or the day care center or the whatever, and that's the proof. If you do a range of those products, then that's the proof that you have the generalized capacity. And then the question is "How do you recognize that before the demonstration of the product?" The closest I come in the intervention I'm looking at…is "When you have an issue that affects this community, you will know somebody to call." So there's a competency element to it and a connectedness.

Even at the individual level, where measures of "capacity" might be easier to track than at the institutional or community level, there is a strong sense among initiative participants that the accomplishments of a CCI will go unobserved by traditional evaluation methods. For example, one governance member described changes in her neighborhood in the following way:

I see different residents begin to expand their involvement, not only within the target community, but outside in the broader community, and I hear key words being used to indicate that they see themselves differently. It's not something funders are probably going to measure and value the way the community does, but it's making a profound difference in the self-image. And once the self-image is corrected or balanced so it's not seen as a deficit, what we're beginning to see is how people show up more powerfully in everything that they do…. So it becomes very broad, and sometimes even almost lost in the myriad of things that people do. But there's a strength there.

This problem of measuring community building has several important costs. One of the most problematic is that outcomes for which there are good measures, such as aggregate-level indicators of infant mortality, teen pregnancy, income, and the like, will be relied upon as the sole indicators of CCI progress. But few expect that the CCI intervention is powerful enough or structured to significantly affect such indicators in the short and medium terms. The danger of focusing inappropriately on measurable "products" is articulated by one director:

> I really believe that the government and the foundations have probably abandoned numerous good interventions simply because global measures were used against particular interventions and absolutely false conclusions were drawn with respect to the consequences. That's a huge danger that I see. The other side of this is then to be very careful about the measures, the order of magnitude to fit an image between what you're actually purporting to measure and the conclusions you're drawing.

The fact that product is so much more easily measured than the effects of process can lead to other problems. In the worst cases, sites may resist evaluation altogether because they believe that evaluators lack the tools to show their progress on the community building front. In other cases, the search for meaningful process indicators may lead evaluators to spend enormous time and energy documenting the CCI's activities, at great expense to the site or the funder. In still other cases, the CCI may redefine its objectives in order to become more readily evaluable by traditional means. One evaluator describes some aspects of these dilemmas:

> The evaluator has been put in a double bind. One, you have to come up with indicators that make sense, you have to go back for clarification on the objective, which becomes a didactic exercise after a while. Pretty soon, you're telling the client, whether you want to or not, hey, it would be a lot easier to measure this thing if you just write it this way.

The challenge to all involved is to be clear about the vision of the CCI and to agree on both process and product outcomes that are linked to that vision. An evaluator describes how agreement about the initiative's objectives can work to produce consensus on measures. In the CCI she is evaluating, all parties have agreed that community building is a core goal:

> It's been very useful in the sense that it allows the initiative to show results of different kinds very quickly, both inside the neighborhoods

and outside the neighborhoods. Because if a group gets itself together, and says "We're the governing body and four months ago we didn't know one another, and today we just held a town meeting and 100 people came," that's a product. And we all know it's a product, and the mayor knows it's a product, she was there, and so on. So it allows you to show results that aren't houses or paved streets or clean lots or whatever.

The Inside-Outside Tension

Comprehensive community initiatives bring together a wide range of actors, including funders, staff, neighborhood stakeholders, technical assistance providers, and evaluators. In bringing these groups together, CCI architects and planners aim deliberately to provide the initiatives with a diversity of experiences, resources, skills, and viewpoints. Given their diversity, it is not surprising that interactions among the various groups are often marked by tension, as actors promote differing perspectives on the goals, principles, and operations of CCIs. Moreover, other dividing lines, such as those between professionals and non-professionals, between residents and non-residents, and between racial and ethnic groups, frequently cross-cut the functional categories and can heighten the intrinsic tension.

When negotiated and balanced, tension of this kind can strengthen and enrich CCIs, as partners draw on each other's backgrounds and capabilities. For example, funders, with their contacts, prestige, and resources, collaborate with neighborhoods to leverage new sources of support, or project directors glean insights from evaluators' perspectives to resolve administrative dilemmas. But this tension can also generate misunderstanding and conflict, as each group tries to assert its particular views about the aims and strategies of the initiative.

Much of the tension generated by these differing perspectives can be understood as the tension between "inside" and "outside," a geographically based metaphor that reflects an "us" and "them" distinction. Connection to the neighborhood is usually the standard for insider status, with the phrase characterizing a perceived conjunction of initiative staff, participants, and other residents and stakeholders. The phrase opposes these insiders to those outside the neighborhood, particularly the funder but sometimes also technical assistance providers, evaluators, and others.

In CCIs, there are various configurations of inside and outside, and the dividing line is porous. For example, in hiring staff, initiatives may grapple with whether insider status refers only to neighborhood residency or whether similarities to residents in terms of background, race/ethnicity, and so on also qualify. Comparable definitional questions also arise in developing governance boards, as communities try to pull together an effective mix of members that might include residents, non-residents, professionals, local power brokers, "pillars of the community," and others.

Moreover, the delineations may shift during the course of an initiative or change meaning depending on context. Residents, for example, may differ among themselves but coalesce in opposition to outside technical assistance providers. And there may be differing opinions within groups or crossovers where, for example, a funder's view on an issue coincides more closely with that of residents than with other funders. Still, the metaphor of inside-outside tensions provides a widely recognized, sharply defined, and frequently applicable framework.

Initiative and Funder:
The Paradigmatic Inside-Outside Relationship

The tension in the inside-outside relationship of CCIs and their funders revolves around basic issues of authority, control, responsibility, and accountability. Who holds the balance of power, resources, and leverage to make decisions that are fundamental to the initiative? These issues are especially relevant to CCIs because of their emphasis on concepts such as "empowerment" and "capacity building." After all, who empowers and whose capacity is being built? As one evaluator puts it, "[it] simply reduces down to who the 'we' is."

CCIs are attempting to create a new and different kind of relationship between funders and initiatives: they aim not simply to move control from one side of the relationship to the other, but to draw on the strengths and richness of their diversity, to find ways to achieve collective action, and to work together to effect meaningful change. Yet both sides are acting within a complex set of constraints that emerge from their different constituencies and accountability structures, from their established ways of operating, and from their historical relationships with the actors in the initiative.

As a starting point, most CCIs are initiated and defined, at least in their broad parameters, by their funders, while the role of local initiative staff and participants is to develop the means for enacting the overall vision. The funder usually makes the first move, "inviting" a relationship with the neighborhood through a request for proposals (as in the case of the federal empowerment zones) or through less formal interactions with a particular neighborhood (as in the case of many foundation-funded efforts). But, from the first contact, the relationship can take many forms. As one person describes:

> **On the one hand, the funder comes in and says, "We've got a bunch of money, this is the model, this is what we want you to do, you really aren't important, we are going to pass it through you to accomplish our end, we're going to send technical assistance people in to do it for you, but you don't really matter." That's the one extreme. The other extreme is to throw the money out there, put the money in their hands and say, "Go do it."**

Most residents believe that the initiative should focus on creating the community that the people want, and not the one that the funder envisions. At an extreme, some residents and governance members argue that funder expectations must be clearly stated so the community can decide whether to accept or refuse funding. This view arises out of the sense among some residents that funders can preempt their right to develop their own goals for the community. For example, a resident who also directs the initiative in her neighborhood explains:

> **If someone other than those in the neighborhood brings the vision, then it's not the neighborhood's vision. I think the most valuable thing that a convenor could bring…is money. [But,] the money has to be unfettered by a vision…. There's an assumption that some leader, convenor, like a foundation or a community foundation, has to bring the vision, otherwise it won't be there. Then that would feel to me like manipulation…. Part of me is the resident who feels [like saying], "Quit coming in here and telling us what the vision is. Stop doing it. I don't care how much money you have."**

For their part, funders are increasingly aware of the potential tensions in their relationships with the initiatives, and some are making concerted efforts to work out new roles for themselves in the CCI context. They agree that CCIs must be able to operate with independence, but views on the extent of that independence can vary. Some funders, for example, recognize a need to cede control over local initiatives to governance structures, but argue this must happen within certain bounds or with certain "strings attached." For example, a funder says, "On the decision making…the funder has to back off from control, but…within the framework of principles and expectations." Some initiative staff are sympathetic to this perspective. A project director is realistic about the fact that initiatives must work within the constraints of funders:

> **The fact of the matter is funders in particular are not going to just put some money out and walk away. And so we found ourselves [in a state of] creative tension, negotiating back and forth about what this means, and what is success, and what does the community want. It's really a negotiating process of give-and-take.**

One funder describes trying to evolve a leadership style that is "distinctly not command and control, but sort of call and response and respecting the process above all else and believing in your partners."

Yet despite this self-conscious consideration of their roles, shifting expectations make it difficult for funders to find the right balance in their relationships with initiatives. For example, while the purpose of empowerment is to transform decision-making authority, issues of leadership and responsibility remain for the funders:

> **I think we are abdicating our responsibility if we just say any decision that is made is *ipso facto* correct just because we believe in empower-ment. I think that isn't being fair. It's applying a very different standard than we apply to anybody else in this world, and we have an obligation to hold the collaboratives to very high standards.**

Another funder says that he believes he made a mistake in ceding too much authority in the interest of empowerment, later finding that he had to backtrack and reintroduce the very real constraints under which he was operating. He believes that, for a new kind of partnership to work, funders need to learn how to be up-front about their own goals and limits, and to be clear about the power dynamics in the relationship:

> **There's a tension between being a patron, being in partnership, and having the neighborhood as your client. It's a mistake veering too far into being their patron.... What I mean by that is not being honest enough, frank enough, direct enough about what my expectations were, what they were really accountable for, what were the constraints in the real world...coddling them.**

A variety of stakeholders concur that funders are often unwilling to acknowledge their position of power and the responsibility that accompanies it. In the CCI context, some funders seem to under-estimate how much they dominate the action, either explicitly or behind the scenes, and ignore opportunities to exert influence in a constructive way. Even residents and governance members sometimes express frustration when funders do not live up to their responsibility to ensure accountability, to make sure that funds are being spent according to initiative guidelines and that activities are actually being implemented. In the view of some, funder demands or "strings" may, as an evaluator says, be "consistently positive in their impact" on the initiative. At the same time, requirements are only as good as their constructive enforcement. The evaluator continues, "An important place where the program has gotten off track…has been because the funders didn't hold up their end of the job in insisting that the conditions actually be met."

Funders must think through their own expectations, and then communicate them clearly to the initiative, governance board, community, and others involved in the project. Again, an evaluator comments:

> **A common problem is that the people holding the strings, whether it's the funders or the leader of a major institution, are not clear enough in their own minds what the strings are, what the limitations are…. And so inevitably they don't communicate the limitations clearly to the residents or other people. And when the residents bump up against the limitations, both parties are surprised. The residents feel betrayed, and their trust tends to dissolve rather quickly.**

Overall, however, there is a sense that relinquishing power is more difficult for funders than they admit and that it requires an "enormous mind set change…to really transfer authority to residents and citizens." The central issue, according to many, is whether the most important source of power—control over funding decisions—is to be devolved: "Who controls the money is a very significant factor." This sentiment is echoed by a program director who says, "Let's be real. It's money driving the stuff that we're talking about." Evaluators report that funder ambivalence is common: a funder may state that community empowerment is an objective but then "when the community decides to do something, the funder says, 'No, not that. You're empowered to do the other stuff.'" Initiative staff describe the same dilemma. For example, a project director reports, "One of the issues that we struggle with and we argue about a lot is: you told us this is about empowerment and this was our process, and now you're telling us what to do, and we don't want that."

Initiatives recognize and value the access to resources and the legitimacy that funders can bring. But, at the same time, they are increasingly alert to the tensions that are raised when their definitions, goals, and needs diverge from those of the funder. Moreover, initiatives are increasingly willing and able to point out such tensions as they look for ways to take greater control of what happens in their neighborhoods, essentially looking to renegotiate roles and influence in their relationships with funders. It may be that a shift in the funder-initiative relationship can happen only through the push-and-pull of actors as they try to find effective balance points in the ongoing negotiations over power.

The Inside-Outside Tension in CCI Operations

The inside-outside framework provides a useful lens on how the initiative and the funder engage in ongoing interaction to meet planning and implementation challenges. This section explores inside-outside tensions through three pivotal operational dimensions: technical assistance, evaluation, and governance. These activities, like implementation overall, largely occur within the structural framework of the funder-initiative relationship, with all of its built-in tensions, but other groups of actors are introduced here. This new configuration is more fluid than the funder-initiative relationship: the line dividing insiders and outsiders may shift in the course of implementation processes, changing definitions of who is in and who is out, and actors sometimes share perspectives across group boundaries.

Technical assistance: Expert skills vs. local empowerment. Technical assistance (TA) brings to the fore basic issues of decision-making responsibility and authority. Who should decide who receives TA, at what times, in what ways, and with what content? These issues and their attendant tensions tend to revolve around the relationship of the funder to the rest of the initiative.

A first issue focuses on *how* technical assistance is provided rather than the substantive areas of assistance. When a community feels that technical assistance is imposed by the funder, there are tensions that community members explicitly and clearly articulate. For example, a governance group member recalls such a situation:

> [The] hard part was that the community felt that the person was being pushed on them, so they pushed back and said, "No!" And so that caused a problem. The TA wasn't weaned into the community…and so there was a push.… It was a rebellion by the community.

A funder characterizes the imposition of technical assistance on initiatives as "forced marriages," and comments that even when such a marriage works, "it was still forced on them by a funder and it just is an endless uphill climb." Resistance to imposed technical assistance reflects the desire of initiatives for autonomy and their vigilance against encroachments by their stronger partners. This resistance is intensified when an initiative interprets the introduction of a consultant as a means for the funder to meet its own needs, and not necessarily those of the initiative in the community.

Questions also arise concerning the appropriate use of technical assistance in community-empowering initiatives and about the ways in which technical assistance is practiced. For example, a governance member describes the reaction of some residents to technical assistance:

[If] TA comes in and facilitates everything…people don't contribute, they don't share their ideas. And what happens…is that when the funding dries up or shifts, people drop out of it because there was no ownership at the neighborhood-based level.

One funder notes the conflict of aims when funders bring "highly skilled technical people from outside into a process that is at the same time empowering local residents." An observer points to the same conflict, arguing that technical assistance providers are likely to want to take over and perform the task at hand. "If you're a technical assistance provider, you end up wanting to do stuff. That's what technical assistant people, consultants, do. They do stuff." Funders can reinforce the TA provider's impulse to "do stuff" when, as contracting agents, they define task completion as a measure of TA success.

This is not to argue that technical assistance has no place in an initiative. Certainly, both initiative participants and funders recognize the need for communities to broaden their horizons, deepen local capacity, and have recourse to technical expertise. However, many agree that the process of decision making concerning technical assistance must change. At the least, CCI actors agree that funders and communities must work together in technical assistance ventures. A responsible funder can, for example, help the community think through the logistics for technical assistance, including criteria for selecting a provider, ways to use a consultant, benchmarks for performance, and appropriate fee levels. As a governance member says, "We needed a way to know what we needed." But many emphasize that such help should not include selecting the provider or deciding what needs to be done. Their view is that the more control the initiative has over the process, the better it will use the TA.

Evaluation: Imported standards vs. local goals. Evaluation is an area that is particularly ripe for inside-outside tensions between funders and initiatives. Evaluators often feel caught in these tensions as they try simultaneously to meet the demands of funders and to walk the fine line in the neighborhood between evaluation and technical assistance provision. Many of the tensions in evaluation relate not so much to the technical aspects of developing new methodologies, but to the social and political meanings of evaluations, and, not surprisingly, to the different ways in which stakeholders define initiative success. These different agendas have the potential to create a sense of frustration and distrust, not only between the funder and the initiatives, but between evaluators and both funders and initiatives. As a staff member says:

> One of the things that we are learning is that evaluation is a double-edged sword. While they provide you with phenomenal management information...they can slit your throat with funders,...[because] the funding community is not very lenient when it comes to mistakes.... No one has yet figured out the formula for success in community transformation and development, so we've got to have this margin of error where we can make some mistakes. We don't know how to do it right yet, folks, and we need to be able to have the luxury of learning how to do that. The evaluations are not going to be valuable if we pay for them with the foundation funding and then slide them into a drawer because they don't say what we want them to say. They're only valuable if you take what's told to you and you do something about it. And you can't do that if you don't get any more money.

Defining success: Demonstrable impact vs. intimate benefits. In part, the mistrust between local initiative actors and funders is rooted in differing perspectives on the meaning of "real change." Outside support often carries with it funder expectations for success for the initiative, and the exercise of assumed decision-making prerogatives on this front. Ironically, the innovative nature of CCIs may be leading some funders to place more emphasis on controlling how CCI success should be defined. As one evaluator comments, "The more experimental and the riskier the investment, the hungrier [funders] are for clear and concise accomplishments." An observer notes that, because CCIs have long-term perspectives and seek new ways of doing business, there is a need to "demonstrate that what we're all about is making a difference, is having a positive impact."

But initiative success means different things to different people, and is another flash point for tensions in the inside-outside relationship. A funder explains that one of the main criteria he faces when he makes a funding decision revolves around showing his board and others that their dollars were well spent:

The real test is how we explain and support that this is about good investment. I have faith, I do have faith, that it ultimately can be done, but I think that it is a very, very difficult challenge. And, can it can be done in a way that is acceptable to outside skeptical policy makers who are going to say, "Show me"?

In part, the role of foundations and, by extension, of individual funders is to make things happen, to catalyze change. Some warn that this can lead to a personalization of the initiative, saying, "The sad reality is …funders are very insecure. Each one of them wants to put a label on their accomplishments of something." They point to the fact that new program officers tend to set new priorities and redefine success for an initiative. Some push for funders to admit explicitly that they are not simply providing funds, but looking for their own rewards as well. For example, a resident involved in governance says, "The funder is a customer. He's getting something for giving you a certain amount of money…. Let's be honest,…[he wants] a feather in [his] cap." Others believe that funders simply want to be associated with success, pointing, for example, to the wish of sponsors to join an initiative once it has been deemed effective. Interwoven throughout is the competitiveness among foundations to support initiatives that are perceived as groundbreaking and consequential.

Funders, therefore, look for change that has policy-level resonance. Such an aim may lead funders to a focus on substantive areas or abstracted goals, such as comprehensiveness, that may not be perceived as matching the needs of communities. For example, an evaluator, in discussing how uninspiring the notion of comprehensiveness is to many, says: "I think poor people struggling to put something together in a community have a shorter tolerance for generalization [i.e., comprehensiveness] than paid professionals," but they cannot follow their own inclinations "because it's the paid professionals who are setting the terms."

The aim to show success may also lead to large-scale expectations that residents feel are impossible to meet. A resident and community activist argues, "You can't expect to put a couple of hundred thousand dollars into a community like my community for a one-year period or an 18-month period and…create this utopia." But such expectations may become part of the "rhetoric" or "hype" about the program. And, in fact, this rhetoric may be used not only by funders to trumpet the foundation's intentions, but also in the neighborhood to arouse the interest of residents, often a difficult process. A challenge may arise if the initiative does not meet these lofty expectations within the time frame. Who will be held accountable? The community that did not achieve the goals or the funder who over-promised?

Some funders, however, disagree with the contention that they focus only on evaluation numbers. They concur that it is inappropriate to look for outcomes in the early years of an initiative, when participants are building infrastructure and laying the groundwork for future development. Others argue that they are careful to admit the limits of their knowledge and to curb expectations:

> We're very clear about the fact that this is a big experiment. And we're putting money into a whole lot of new things, many of which probably won't work or probably won't work in achieving the desired outcomes, and we're learning and we're experimenting.... We've said, "Let's get this down to real common sense, plain talk, honest expectation-setting about what we can and can't do. And the fact that this is an experiment."

For their part, neighborhood-based CCI actors often have a working definition of success that differs both in substance and in contextual roots from that of funders. They argue that when evaluations focus on long-term outcomes, they neglect changes that are very real, but are not easily measured, such as declines in the level of social isolation, growing social integration, or changing attitudes toward the community. Similarly, although community-based neighborhood initiative actors may argue that capacity-building and other types of learning should be seen as a critical outcome, they believe that funders do not want to hear about such lessons. Rather, according to some local staff, funders take a narrow view:

> [Funders want] to know whether you met the numbers or didn't meet the numbers. And I think we learn a lot, but nobody wants to learn from us in the neighborhoods. They just want to see—" Okay, you said you were going to build 24 houses. Did you build 24 houses?" They don't want to know that we're now experts in soil remediation.

Resident definitions of success also have a more personal impetus where the difficulty of life in the neighborhood and the suffering of residents becomes a touchstone and point of authority for those in the neighborhood. This also becomes the basis for arguing that residents, who will be most affected by the initiative, know best what needs to be done and how to do it. For example, when describing the governance process in one initiative, a resident says, "A lot of times we find when you bring people in who don't live there, who don't go through the aches and pains like we do as residents, [they] aren't as sensitive...as we are." Such experiential knowledge cannot, of course, be fully shared by outsiders, but initiative staff and participants in the neighborhood increasingly demand that it be respected by funders and other outsiders, such as technical assistance providers and evaluators, for whom the ability to work well with neighborhood people is increasingly important.

At the same time, this experiential knowledge leads to different measures and meanings for initiative success. A governance member says:

People in my neighborhood are…gaining some personal, very intimate kinds of benefits. They don't care whether it's on paper; they don't care whether you can count it or whether you can touch it. It's more of an emotional thing that they feel that change has taken place on that level, and that's equally valuable.

The notion of intimacy of benefits is pivotal in grasping differences among definitions of success, and must be taken into account in efforts to reconcile these meanings. A funder reiterates how the degree of closeness to the initiative gives rise to different perspectives on whether change has occurred, and therefore on the question of success. The farther people are from the neighborhood, he says, the less convinced they are that something has happened: the initiatives are "convinced that they're making a huge difference in the neighborhood" and funders are the least convinced. "It might be that unless you're close enough to the action to see, feel, and touch what's going on, you aren't going to be convinced and you never will be, because there aren't going to be these wonderful quantifiable things that are going on."

The evaluator's role: Serving the funder vs. engaging local participants. Tensions over the focus of evaluation efforts can give rise to pressure on evaluators. Within the initiative-funder relationship, such pressure may place evaluators on the boundary between insider and outsider status. On the one hand, as discussed above, funders frequently rely on evaluators for assessment of the progress of initiatives, justification of the investment of resources, and ammunition in broader policy deliberations. This reliance, and especially perceived evaluator responsiveness to it, can place evaluators clearly outside the community. Thus, for example, local initiative actors and residents may see evaluations as giving "the foundations what they want to hear. That's their return on their investment." Underscoring this perception of at least some evaluation efforts, an observer points out that at times the evaluator's job is to provide a favorable report on the funding manager's performance: "There are a lot of hired guns out there who practice from that perspective." Somewhat less cynically, an evaluator describes the demands of his role and, in doing so, sums up many of the difficulties of an intermediary caught in inside-outside tensions:

> As an evaluator...[I find that funders are] pressing you to one degree or another to say things that don't exist in reality. They then sometimes turn to you as a TA provider and say, "I know you couldn't say this and evaluate it. Could you make it happen as a TA provider? You know, I want to be 70 percent of the way there. Why don't you give me some TA, then we'll be 70 percent there. Then you can tell me we are." And so, you have to find two different ways...from two different roles for telling them the fantasy and the reality.

Some participants defend the funders' emphasis on wanting to show real change. They argue that foundation program officers are committed to improving lives and promoting community well-being and feel that their role is to help press all the players on. One evaluator describes how this plays out for him:

> The degree of suffering that we look at, and...that our funders look at, and think about, and care about when they look at these communities is almost more than anyone can think about. And what we have to tell them about what happens in the alleviation of that suffering is unacceptable in some way. Not enough, obviously. And so, we can never give the right news.

Some suggest that these divergent definitions of real change and of valid measures could be reconciled if funders incorporated initiative perspectives into the evaluation design. In fact, if a participatory process for defining evaluation methods and measures is used, it could reduce the various tensions within an initiative, especially the "us" vs. "them" nature of the evaluation enterprise. One governance member tells of his CCI's experience, where the evaluator held training sessions for board members and steering committee members to talk about evaluation and "the resentment and ambivalence or whatever kind of died down because we understood what he was doing." The group turned to discussions of how they could use the evaluator's "impartial, detached view of the way things are going" to the ongoing benefit of the initiative. One longtime observer of the field suggests that a collaborative's ability to perceive evaluation in this constructive and non-threatening way may be, in itself, an evaluation point, and one of the best measures of collaborative functioning.

In these cases, evaluations are "learning instruments" and are useful for feedback and for ongoing program development. Here an evaluator can play a pivotal role in the relationship of the initiative and funder, providing an effective and constructive intermediary ground between inside and outside. For example, a director says:

> **Some of my experiences with evaluators, both local and national, that I value the most are when I can just sit and have another person to brainstorm with. Often, you know, I find myself without a real peer in town to talk to. Either they're a collaborative member, a committee member, a grantee, a funder, a board member, or an employee. So to be able to sit and talk with someone else who is looking at the big picture has been incredibly helpful.**

Here, as at other critical inside-outside junctures in the practice of CCIs, there is a need to balance the tensions of multiple perceptions and multiple claims to initiative ownership. In terms of evaluation, this seems to call for weighing and negotiating a need for outcomes with a willingness to allow initiatives room to rethink strategies based on evaluation findings.

Governance: Representativeness vs. effectiveness. There is consensus among all CCI stakeholders about the need to include neighborhood residents on governance boards. The vision and perspectives that residents can bring "really reflect the needs of the neighborhood." This view is strongly espoused by neighborhood residents participating in CCIs. They view their involvement in all aspects of the decision-making and management processes as critical to a CCI's quest to become a legitimate actor in the neighborhood and to achieve sustainable change.

Some argue the case in historical terms: given the fact that many initiatives in the past have disenfranchised neighborhood people, CCIs have to fight skepticism by working explicitly to engage residents and other stakeholders:

When you constantly come and bring issues and bring programs and
bring plans without involving people, you don't get the kind of
excitement or you don't get the kind of feedback you need to get. People
have become so apathetic in the community, you could come in with a
truck of gold and put it down there and say "this is going to be for this
community," and people are not going to budge, because they were not
involved in the process.

Yet, some raise issues around who actually constitutes and represents
the community. For example, a governance participant says:

Non-profits tend to think they are the community, because their boards
are made up of community people, or their staff. But really, as a whole,
non-profits are not the community. They may be the keepers of the
vision…but their decisions aren't necessarily the right decisions unless
they're community driven…. You need to look at the people who are
living there [in the neighborhood] every single day. They're the ones who
are the community.

Therefore, CCIs place emphasis on ensuring that a range of different
organizational and individual interests are represented, and that
deliberate efforts are made to ensure that residents' perspectives are
included.

There are…three levels of players in a lot of [CCIs]. There are the
neighborhood residents or parents, sort of the grassroots level, on the
one end. At the other end, there's the systems level, represented by
perhaps the medical center, or school district, or county. And then in the
middle there are all those non-profit providers, whether they're CDCs or
social service agencies. And increasingly it's become clear…[that the]
provider level and the systems level have to get out of the way…and let
the community or the parents…"find their own voice." If they can't do
that without being pushed around or intimidated by the other two
levels, then nothing happens.

Within a single geographic community there are usually several
subcommunities, each with its own interests and needs, and a CCI
board might be made up of representatives of all of them. The self-
interest that they inevitably bring to their positions as board members
can create problems. But several initiatives can point to times when the
governance structure has proven to be an effective vehicle for working
successfully through these differences.

We decided that self-interest is not a bad thing. It's there, it's what drives
a lot of us to do what we do. But let's just put it out on the table and talk

about what our self-interest is, why we're in this, and then begin to find ways in which [our separate interests] connect.

Racial and ethnic diversity in a neighborhood adds yet another level of complexity to the challenge of creating a working governance structure in neighborhoods. Almost all CCIs are located in neigh-borhoods made up predominantly of people of color. In neighborhoods where there is a second or third significant minority group, residents and governance members have generally made efforts to ensure that all racial/ethnic groups participate in the governance of the initiative with varying degrees of success. One director describes how her initiative adopted a mechanistic strategy for dealing with the problem:

> **There's also a danger when we talk about residents [that we're] somehow assuming homogeneity there. There's tremendous variation. In [our city], we literally establish quotas of representation by different cultural communities, not based on percentage of the population but just on existence.... We found [that] we need such compensatory measures to keep the normally dominant group from just sort of taking over.**

In addition to the consensus about including neighborhood residents, there is strong consensus about aiming for diversity among governance board members. This may begin with the simple extension of governance boards to include non-residents. For example, a governance member argues that "a neighborhood is part of a larger community" and any group composed only of neighborhood people will have a difficult time running a CCI. Relevant "outsiders" may include people with "political clout," representatives of local government, outsiders who can contribute a perspective "from a distance," technical assistance providers, and others. The critical issue may be, in the end, a shared stance toward change. But this does not come naturally. It generally requires a lot of hard work to break down barriers and build a common vision. For example, initial differences in experience, styles of self-presentation, and knowledge of bureaucratic niceties and strategies may make it difficult for resident voices to be expressed, listened to, and heeded.

While the value of resident participation is widely stressed, there is some concern about the possible costs associated with emphasizing resident involvement. Some CCI participants, including some who might be viewed as on the "outside," argue that outsiders will not fully attend to the views of residents until initiatives either prepare them to sit at the governance table or structure the board in such a way that residents are deliberately over-represented. An observer sums up this sentiment: "What we haven't done is enhance the capacity of people in the neighborhood…to be able to come to the table as equals to leverage their particular [perspective]." In a statement that brings together issues of representativeness and effectiveness, a governance member underlines the desirability for diversity in counterpoint to a funder's sole focus on grassroots participation:

> **Another problem that we had in the beginning was the fact that our funders pretty much mandated that the board be totally grassroots people from the neighborhood…. And what we ran into is…we had board members who had no earthly idea what it meant to actually sit on a board and make those kinds of decisions.**

Such difficulties involving residents, especially those without governance experience, also crop up in comments of those responsible for managing initiatives. Directors and staff cite instances, for example, when board members do not "know the difference between policy decisions and management decisions," or "want to be the administrator as well as the policy maker." Here, training of neighborhood people for participation on governance boards goes beyond issues of style to include clarity about the role of the board and how it functions.

At the same time, some residents and staff point out that learning has to occur on the other side of the table as well. As a staff member argues, "We have a lot of opinions, but they don't listen to us. They don't care whether we're sitting in the room or not. They expect us to just nod, because they don't think that we have anything to say." A resident describes the difficult coming together of residents and outsiders:

> **Bringing people who live in…[middle-class neighborhoods] to come in and sit at the table with neighborhood people when they've never done it before, you've got a credibility issue there. "What do these people know even though that's their neighborhood? They don't know anything because they don't have the education to understand, to know what they need." So, it took a long time for even respect to come across the table.**

A staff person underscores the need for work on both sides of the table if CCI actors are to overcome inside-outside tensions and work effectively as a team: "[It's] not just preparing residents to be able to sit in there and fight, you know, but you have to reform the boards and the agencies themselves in terms of whether they respect people and think that they have something to say."

Over time, as the initiative itself creates—or at least appears to create—differential access to influence and opportunity, membership in the governance structure may cause the lines defining inside and outside to shift. CCIs aim to develop local capacity and encourage local leadership. Yet, in an ironic twist, some residents may perceive emerging local leaders in a different light, redefining them as outsiders. A resident comments, for example, "If you put on a coat and tie, you may no longer be perceived as 'one of us.'" Another resident and project director describes an approach he hopes can counteract such changing perceptions:

> **If you're grounded, there's that respect that's accorded to you throughout the community, even though they might see you one day on TV with your shirt and tie on standing next to the mayor. The next day, they see you with your tennis shoes and your jogging suit on standing down there.... They see you walking through the neighborhood. They see you carrying your groceries home.... But if they don't see you, then you disconnect yourself from the folks you purport to work with and for.**

Finally, having invested in the process and developed a strong neighborhood identity, initiative participants believe that they have a stronger base from which to deal with the outside community. Traditional organizers have long promoted the notion that an organized neighborhood is a more powerful neighborhood, and the community building dimension of CCIs is based in part on that philosophy. Some of the proudest moments of CCIs have come when the neighborhood has had an impact on an outside event or the actions of an outside entity. Examples include getting the city to respond to the problem of illegal dumping in the neighborhood, voting in record numbers for Hispanic public officials, co-investing with a development company in the creation of an industrial park at the edge of the neighborhood, and encouraging a major bank to locate a branch in a neighborhood. As one governance member explained:

> **It's not a bunch of professionals and reformers changing the local school. It's the parents and the seniors in that community taking on the principal in that school, and building with another school, [and so on].**

Despite complications and difficulties, local governance provides CCIs with a potential means for meeting a complex challenge that is intrinsic to CCIs: to negotiate authority, control, responsibility, and accountability across a range of actors who come together to effect deep, meaningful, and lasting change. In some ways, the tensions inherent in the dynamics of CCIs reflect tensions in any bureaucratic undertaking, but they may be intensified by CCIs' deliberate aim to shift and reshape decision-making processes. It is in this endeavor that governance boards, with their emphases on collaboration, representativeness, and inclusion, may be pivotal in providing what one observer describes as "the choreography of effective leadership and management."

3

Getting Started:
Findings from CCI Practice

As the previous chapter suggests, few of the lessons that are being learned about CCIs are one-dimensional. They are difficult to pinpoint because they depend on the history and culture of the neighborhood, the context in which the initiative is being developed, the funder's priorities and constraints, the technical resources that are made available, and so on. CCIs are dynamic enterprises that strive to balance various agendas and resources in order to produce neighborhood change. The reader should bear in mind, therefore, that many lessons that are being learned about CCI goals, principles, and operational strategies are best understood within the context of the process-product and inside-outside tensions discussed in chapter 2.

In addition, because the CCI phenomenon is still young, lessons based on experience are necessarily limited to those that surround the earliest decisions made by CCI architects, planners and sponsors. This chapter highlights findings about CCI goals, principles, operations, and programs that appear to be emerging from this early experience. These findings should not be seen as seen as all that is to be learned about operations in the field of CCIs. Most of what there is to learn about CCIs remains to be unveiled as the field matures.

Goals for Change

The CCI phenomenon is still too young to support conclusions about whether the initiatives will achieve the magnitude of change to which they aspire at the individual/family, neighborhood, and system levels. Therefore, this report cannot shed light on whether the CCI inter-vention is powerful enough to deliver on its considerable promise. It can, however, highlight the fact that those who are currently engaged in

55

GETTING

STARTED:

FINDINGS

FROM

CCI

PRACTICE

CCIs believe strongly in their potential. This is true across the board, and includes funders, directors and staff, evaluators, governance members, neighborhood residents, and even skeptical outside observers of the field. They see the CCI movement as one that has learned from past mistakes about the importance of integrating programmatic efforts, linking individual and community change, engaging residents, creating partnership between communities and powerful forces beyond their borders, and building capacity at many levels to sustain positive change over the long run. They see the CCI as a vehicle that incorporates these lessons and applies them in new ways in order to determine "what works" for their neighborhoods.

At the same time, for CCIs, it appears that certain ways to approach change are more easily defined, planned for, and implemented. For example, strategies for improving individual- and family-level outcomes seem to be the most straightforward, probably because many of the institutions participating in the initiative process on the ground are experienced service providers. Individual change that pertains to less concrete outcomes, notably leadership development, is somewhat more complicated and is discussed in more detail below in the section on community building.

Each higher level of change appears to bring with it greater challenges. Most participants are keenly aware of the obstacles to achieving neighborhood transformation. At the same time, neighborhood-level change that revolves around physical revitalization and, to a somewhat lesser extent, economic development feels familiar to the CCI enterprise since the experience of the community development corporation movement feeds directly into CCIs. Neighborhood-level change that focuses on strengthening community capacity and associational ties, on the other hand, is an area where knowledge is only now being generated.

System-level change appears to be the most difficult agenda for CCIs to articulate programmatically. The difficulty may stem in part from inside-outside tensions around definitions and priorities. A number of insiders feel that systems change is "too much of a burden" for CCIs, and that they are being set up to fail if it becomes the major criterion for success. Systems change, in this view, should be the long-term consequence of neighborhood transformation, not its driving objective:

We can have systems change and planning and process at any level you choose, but ultimately, if you can't deliver it at the local level in the neighborhoods to individuals, all the rest is worthless. And so the emphasis to me, the focus has to be on building capacity at the neighborhood level, if it isn't there, and nurturing it, if it is there. And then the other levels will take care of themselves as that bubbles up. Systems and programs [will] change…incrementally over time in response to real issues and real programs and real people that are taking place at the local level. I think the effort to come in from above in an abstract way and say "we need to change the system" simply leads to meetings and papers and not much real change down at the local level.

Some observers of the field believe that systems change must be a primary focus for CCIs. They suggest that the generous and flexible foundation funding that CCIs have received may have protected them from having to deal directly with these larger issues thus far. But, they argue, if CCIs have ambitions to achieve large scale change, they cannot avoid policy and system reform. In the words of one observer, "Change insulated from the 'systems downtown' is nothing but therapy."

Reforming and integrating such systems as welfare, employment and training, and housing requires a particular timeline, the investment of specific players, and a certain amount of broad political will at the top. These characteristics may not be compatible with a neighborhood-level strategy that puts a high value on resident participation and ownership. Indeed, some system reform efforts present neighborhoods with a "reformed" system, treating the neighborhood more as an administrative entity, a place in which the reform will occur, than as a participant in the change process. In this case, the reforms play out in neighborhoods but they are not embraced—and are sometimes undermined—by the neighborhood residents and organizations who are the intended beneficiaries. According to this perspective, neighborhood-driven initiatives are not well positioned to lead a systems change effort, but they can be important partners in a broader change process:

These initiatives shouldn't _do_ systems change but they should surface the key reforms that need to be done to the system, so that those who are placed to promote them have grounded information about what should be done.

57

GETTING

STARTED:

FINDINGS

FROM

CCI

PRACTICE

Core Principles in Action

CCIs continue to struggle with the challenge of defining the core principles of comprehensiveness and community building in terms that promote effective action. Because of their breadth, these principles have been useful in establishing fundamental commitments but they have not necessarily facilitated the creation of immediate agendas for change.

Comprehensiveness

Recent experience in the initiatives suggests that the principle of comprehensiveness—defined as a requirement to achieve individual/ family, neighborhood, and systems change in the physical, economic, and social sectors—has not proven a useful guide for action. It is too broad and difficult to operationalize for a variety of reasons, including such practical considerations as the constraints in staffing and resources faced by CCIs. As one participant in the peer group discussions describes:

> While we use the phrase, "comprehensive community initiatives," if you use a dictionary definition of "comprehensive," which I assume means something like "all-inclusive, everything," something like that—none of these initiatives can possibly be comprehensive at the community level, with [the resources that they have available]. Neighborhoods are such complex institutions and a foundation-funded intervention, even with a lot of leveraging, can make an important difference. But is it really comprehensive? I'm increasingly wondering.

Moreover, the notion can be paralyzing: addressing the full spectrum of needs and circumstances at once is an impossible task, and the freedom to do everything does not help clarify the basis for making strategic choices. As one evaluator points out, comprehensiveness may represent an overreaction to the failure of categorical approaches. While a broad, permissive vision avoids limiting an initiative, it also gives little guidance as to what an initiative *will* accomplish:

> It is important for people, as they envision new and different ways of combining actions and groups of people and institutions, to somehow not lose—to demand of themselves—a level of clarity about both what is being done and the impact it will have on people's lives as early as possible. The [comprehensive] vision is very seductive.

Although the notion of comprehensiveness may not have proven useful in moving the initiatives forward, particularly in the short term, most of the discussion group participants support the articulation of a comprehensive vision if it is understood as an "ideal" or a "developmental process"—a way to frame the long-term objectives of the initiative. Thus, in the words of one participant, comprehensiveness is better and most usefully understood as "permissiveness: a lens that allows you the freedom to pick strategically for community-building purposes." That is, it frees an initiative from categorical constraints, allows a range of strategies to be explored, and enables actors to take advantage of opportunities as they come up. Understood as the "absence of limitations," therefore, comprehensiveness allows initiative stakeholders to develop and pursue their own vision of what is needed in their community.

There are conditions that facilitate implementation of a comprehensive approach, including a flexible funding base that supports comprehensive activity, local capacity to move away from categorical planning and implementation, technical support to aid in the building of linkages across projects, development of a broad strategic plan, and identification of a clear starting point from which to launch the plan.

Community Building

The CCI field is, in many respects, defining the meaning of "community building" as it goes along. In an effort to reflect current thinking and practice, this document offers a definition that focuses on building capacity in neighborhood institutions, strengthening ties among residents, and developing individual capacities in order to work individually and collectively toward neighborhood change. This section describes how the definition is playing out at this stage of the CCI movement.

Capacity building in the neighborhood. The capacity building dimension of the CCI enterprise is front and center for all initiatives. As one participant explains, CCIs are "not about solving any particular problems like child care or drugs or whatever, but about generalized problem solving capability, which to me implies a collection of people…and an ability to reach out to the outside." In the words of another respondent:

> **What we're talking about…is the long-term agenda of building the capacity in these communities to take on whatever agenda pops up.… We're talking about trying to get to the point where you really have a group that is accountable, or a group of groups that are accountable, to people in the neighborhood, that can really run with an agenda and have results that benefit people.… It's building that ability of a community to**

59

GETTING
STARTED:
FINDINGS
FROM
CCI
PRACTICE

> set a vision and go for opportunities and actually produce results. That's
> what community building is.

But, as discussed in chapter 2, an emphasis on capacity building sometimes means re-prioritizing programmatic strategies. As one resident explains:

> You have to hear what the community is saying. And although they may
> have an idea that they want to put a fence around a playground, that may
> not be important to you. You may be saying "'My God, we have economic
> development problems here, we have health problems here, and all
> you're interested in is a fence?" Well, if we can help you get that fence,
> you will see that accomplishment. And once you have that feeling that,
> "Hey, I gave this idea and it was successful," then we begin to pull you
> in more.

A commonly held view is that while any particular product that emerges from the work of a CCI is surely valuable, what is more important is the feeling that "we figured that if we could do that one thing, we could do some other things in our community too." Thus, the capacity building element of the community building agenda is an area where thinking among all stakeholders appears to be converging.

Strengthening social networks. Strengthening social networks, both formal and informal, among residents is a high priority in CCIs. Some place priority on strengthening social relationships because of a strong belief in the power of social-organizational forces at the neighborhood level to affect individual outcomes. In this case, neighborhood-level change may be an end in itself, but it is also seen as a vehicle to improve individual lives, as illustrated in this comment:

> We think there is something about the overall set of values that's out
> there in the street and in the community that also has an effect on
> whether people become teenage parents, whether they get a job,
> whether they have a work ethic. A lot of things of that kind are collective
> values, and that's one of the things that community building is about....
> Are there block parties? Do people come out for meetings? Is it safe to
> go out on the street? Do people help each other with things? These
> in my lexicon have an intrinsic validity to them and are part of what
> community is about. At the same time we think that they also may pay
> off in people's individual outcomes as well.

For others, the associational aspects of community building are key. These might be accomplished through informal means, as illustrated in this comment:

I really resonate toward the relationships, the new relationships that are built. I asked the residents who sit around the steering committee table every time we meet, "How many new people did you talk to about this neighborhood plan since last time we met?" That's something to measure. There's where you're beginning to get people talking about neighborhood revitalization and what they can contribute to that process.... You need to do something, whether it's build a fence or get rid of illegal dumping. You can do leadership development, you can do technical assistance, you can do a whole lot of research and study... around what you do, but it's those relationships that are going to last. And it's that information that you share with others that's going to be transferred and cycled back and forth again and again.

Community building through association can also be pursued more formally:

So when we talk about community building, one level that I see is that we have created this very tangled network now of our church network and our nonprofit network. And it's kind of like these strings that go all across the neighborhood. And everybody in our neighborhood is somehow connected to one of those strings that are hanging down.

One participant reports that his collaborative started screening projects at all levels for the potential to set in motion something that strengthens "social capital" and "civic participation." The aim is generally to strengthen both affective and instrumental ties between people. In other words, individuals benefit from both the emotional and psychological support that they get from relationships with others as well as from the social supports, access to information, access to opportunity, and so on.

An important aspect of working to strengthen relationships among people in some CCI neighborhoods is building cross-racial and cross-cultural communication, trust, and collective action. Some CCIs have developed strategies for promoting inclusiveness, but progress on this front needs to be monitored.

Leadership development. Even at this early stage in CCI history, participants can report in depth about how the leadership development process works and its impact. Leadership development has emerged as a fundamental element, both because of its role in improving the life circumstances of individuals and because it is a central aspect of the community building process. In the CCI context, leadership development is seen as "supporting people through the slow process of

61

GETTING

STARTED:

FINDINGS

FROM

CCI

PRACTICE

building confidence and self-esteem" and strengthening their perceived ability to influence the events affecting their lives. One participant notes that when people see themselves as failures, they don't want to become involved and risk being judged by others. They are too vulnerable: "Parents don't come to the PTA because they don't want to feel stupid."

Leadership development is a particular priority for CCI participants who are residents or otherwise very close to the neighborhood. As one CCI staff person who is also a resident explains: "I hope not to be doing this ten years from now. I hope somebody else sits there, who's maybe 15 or 20 years old now, who can sit up and say, 'Hey, we're taking this vision to an even higher level.'" They speak powerfully about how developing and supporting leaders is a "one-on-one" process that requires holding people's hands, bringing them to meetings, and reinforcing the message that they are important and needed. They describe how disempowered people need to develop trust and to feel secure enough and have the confidence to become involved in more significant ways.

> **You have to begin with someone feeling good enough about themselves to take a risk. And that's at the very bottom of it and that's where new leadership comes from. Now, you could take someone that already grew up with a high level of confidence and self-esteem, but that's not what we're really all about. We're about moving people up on the ladder.**

Among residents, there is a high degree of consensus around these views, summarized as, "You cannot empower people. People have to empower themselves." Perhaps the best illustration is the personal story of one woman who is now a resident and leader in one the CCI neighborhoods:

> **I can remember vividly when I was right here in New York State, when I was seventeen years old, with a teenage husband and two children. And I was in the migrant stream in a little place called Pooleville, New York.... There was a day care center nearby and my two babies were in the day care center, and I would take them there and get ready and go to the bean field, come back, and get my children out of day care.**
>
> **The nurse would come around the camp at night, you know, to see the children's shot record and physicals, or to talk to you about the children.... This was a big problem, you know, having parents hold onto shot records or be able to produce them at the time or even take the children to get them.... The nurse was impressed with me because I was**

so young but yet I had my shot records and I had my children up to date. She was so impressed with that that she would come to me and ask me if I would walk around to talk to the other mothers in the camp.

I would do that with her [the nurse], whenever she'd come.... And somehow or another she talked to the day care people and said that she thought it would be a good idea if they would hire me to be an aide over there, maybe help with lunch and this and that...so I could be a link between the parents and the center. They hired me to be an aide...and my whole life changed...because I realized that there was something that I could do to help somebody. I felt so good about it and I wanted to do it. And I've been doing it ever since. Had she not come along to encourage [me] and to let me know that I was valuable, that I have something to offer, I probably would have been in the [migrant] stream today.

CCIs are, in effect, opportunity structures within which new leaders can emerge and be supported. Leaders can grow within the organization as employees, board members, task force members, participants in community meetings, interns, and volunteers. Most CCIs have adopted staffing strategies that deliberately involve neighborhood residents and provide them with opportunities to take on greater responsibility over time. As one director states:

That's really been, I think, the greatest thing about this—that we do have a continuous and ongoing training system for residents and we have been able to hire residents.... [Part of our] very competent staff are two young men who grew up in the neighborhood and who have learned the job, have been with the initiative six years now and are really leaders from the community...but they started out as trainees under someone else in the job.

One CCI has adopted a strategy of "parallel staffing" for leadership development. In parallel staffing, a deputy with growth potential is brought in to work alongside a highly qualified senior person to learn from him or her on a daily basis. "Now that has cost implications and management implications and sometimes race implications and all kinds of implications, but the fact of the matter is that the only way to grow capacity is to take time to nurture it."

Over and over again, participants at all levels of CCIs spoke of "people waiting to be asked" to participate in some capacity, and of the challenge of ensuring that initiatives reach out to new people on a continuous basis:

63

GETTING

STARTED:

FINDINGS

FROM

CCI

PRACTICE

> One of the really important things that I see happening is an emergence of new leaders. I think that what happens in a lot of poor communities is there's a sort of core group of people, and they're on the advisory board of this, and then you go to the police station meeting, and they're over there. And you go to a school board meeting, and they're over there…. And a lot of the potential leaders get missed: that 25-year old single mother with four kids, who's the leader of her tenants' association. And so, I think it is important to give [CCI workers] the opportunity to identify these leaders on the ground, and not really do all the organizing themselves, but really find the leaders to do the organizing.

Few CCIs report having had much success with formal training programs. Several have developed linkages with local universities, where CCI participants are taught technical as well as management and communications skills. Those that incorporate practical experience working within the neighborhood on particular problems appear to have been the most helpful from CCI participants' perspective.

Lessons for Operations

Governance and Establishing an Institutional Base

Across various groups of actors in CCIs, there is agreement about the need to develop a local governance mechanism to carry out a CCI. The form that it takes, however, can vary tremendously according to local circumstances.

The complex nature of the CCI enterprise places special demands on whatever governance structure is put into place for planning and implementing the initiative. In the critical early stages of a CCI, the question of instrumentality tends to focus around the choice of working through an existing organization, or "lead agency," such as a community development corporation or a service agency, or creating a new mechanism such as a collaborative board or coalition.

One side of the argument suggests that working through a strong existing organization in the neighborhood, with a professional staff and the best technical assistance that foundation money can buy, is the most strategic and effective way to ensure improvements in individual and community circumstances. In the words of one observer: "The anointing of that lead organization may be despotic and autocratic but it is also effective." For example, there are many people who see CDCs as experienced and "pragmatic" organizations that already have the ability to work effectively at the neighborhood level, can "set up very practical governing structures," and know how to get "the important players to the table." As one observer notes, "to try to do a broader based collaborative in a neighborhood where there is an effective CDC…is missing a real opportunity and resource."

But CCI participants at all levels voice cautions about working through a strong lead agency. One important concern is that existing organizations in the community have vested interests to protect, whether they are social service organizations, CDCs, schools, churches, public housing tenant organizations, or even experienced community organizers who might have a more political agenda. As one director recounts: "We went through the [process of asking] is there legitimacy attached to any of these alternatives, and ultimately became convinced that the answer was no, that they all had baggage." Those interests might relate to funding base, political base, or even particular per-sonalities, and it is difficult for an outside organization, such as a funder, to appreciate those intricate relationships.

The second caution is that existing institutions also have an established way of doing business and, therefore, operational constraints to taking on the CCI agenda:

> **Where we see problems is where grants are given to already existing organizations to direct the community development process, but they, in fact, already have their own purpose and mission…. They cannot be expected to adjust, to be inclusive and reach out further.**

This is particularly the case when an initiative, working through a technically sophisticated organization like a CDC, puts the community building agenda on the front burner and expects a change in operating style:

> **The more sophisticated CDCs are not terrific collaborators…. They've kind of gotten used to doing it on their own. And because of their concern with capital and the time value of money and all the things that developers care about, they don't have time. Process is not something they've really done a lot of in the housing development world. And so this notion of partnership—if not total collaboration—is proving to be kind of challenging for them.**

Creating a new collaboration of some form is the other principal governance strategy that CCIs tend to follow. In these instances, there is no one lead agency. Individuals are brought together, sometimes as representatives of their employer agencies and sometimes without formal representational roles, into a new decision-making and

65

GETTING
STARTED:
FINDINGS
FROM
CCI
PRACTICE

management structure. Generally, these structures are made up of residents and non-residents who are perceived to have access to outside resources or power. Their degree of formality varies widely, from temporary ad hoc collaboratives to formal boards that go on to create new, independent 501(c)(3) organizations.

Creating this new form of collaboration is seen as necessary in some of the most depleted neighborhoods, either because they lack strong neighborhood institutions or because those that exist are unlikely to be able to deal with the political, technical, and other demands that a CCI places on an organization. Even where strong institutions do exist, CCI designers may nonetheless choose to create a new collaborative structure as a mechanism for avoiding the problems of entrenched interests and ways of doing business. The new collaborative is seen to allow an initiative to start with a clean slate:

> **If you really want to affect a whole community, to not start with a 501(c)(3), I think, is a better idea. Because you're then, by definition, legally formless. And that gives you some time to actually get to know who's in your community, and not set the rules so tightly on the front end. So I would say some coalition or collaborative structure that's loose enough to be able to get going on things and do a lot of exploratory stuff, to put together a vision, a plan, would be the ideal if you're trying to affect one neighborhood.**

But creating a new collaborative has its costs as well. New collaborations need to develop operating procedures from scratch and they need to earn their legitimacy. The process of creating a new institution, whether formal or informal, is so cumbersome that some feel that its prospects for effecting real change are actually weakened. One observer describes the experience of one community group:

> **They brought together sixty-two agencies, and there was this incredible process. They produced a product, this plan, that had some seventy-three initiatives in there. Most of it pretty do-able, I thought. I mean it was not one of these pie in the sky, let's have a mall and all. It was real stuff. The problem is, they can't get it done. There's the plan, there's all these initiatives, but when they try to decide, okay which one of the seventy-three do we do first, they can't—because it was a consensus thing, because there's really no driving force there except the coalition.**

Moreover, a contrived collaborative may not survive beyond the foundation's funding:

One of the problems with the collaboratives that are created, in response to a funder's initiative, is that they're not very durable.... [In one initiative] it took so darn long for the collaborative to form itself. You know they spent all their time trying to figure out, well, what is it that this funder really wants? And the truth is it was so new for everybody they didn't really know for sure.... But very few of those collaboratives still exist.

Thus, although the question of working through a lead agency versus creating a new collaborative may appear central to those in the early stages of CCI design, a clear conclusion from the experience of CCIs that have been in operation for some time is that the question sets up a false dichotomy. All CCIs are simultaneously working with existing organizations and creating something new. A new collaborative will need to work with existing neighborhood institutions, and an anointed lead agency will be required to interact with the neighborhood in new and different ways. Therefore, if the enormous weight given to the "new vs. existing organization" decision is based on the search for shortcuts on the capacity-building front, it is now clear that few, if any, such shortcuts exist.

The key is to ensure that form and function are well matched, and that one dimension does not get too far out in front of the other. One long-time observer of the field warned that the new CCIs seem to spend too much effort up front tweaking the governance structure, even before the CCI activities are well defined:

In my experience, one mistake that's made in these initiatives is to start first with trying to figure out a structure and process as the first challenge. In the things that I've seen work, whether they're called CCIs or something else, it sort of goes the other way. First, there's a powerful notion or concept or idea somewhere that drives people to action. Then there's leadership that's able to move it forward. And then that leader, working with the powerful idea, defines, creates, makes up, cobbles together, process and structure to suit his or her style and to carry it forth. Now, that's my experience of why and how things work.

Those who are designing the governance structure of a CCI need to have the tools to assess neighborhood circumstances and flexibility to respond to them, so as to maximize the initiative's potential to be comprehensive and to pursue its community building agenda. For example, a new CCI needs to recognize and respect the neighborhood networks that are in place. CCIs are not operating in virgin territory,

67

GETTING

STARTED:

FINDINGS

FROM

CCI

PRACTICE

and in any neighborhood there will be a number of existing organi-zations, many of which will have participated in one or another poverty alleviation or community development initiative in the past. In part because of their foundation or other high profile sponsors, CCIs can too easily fail to involve key local actors. Several CCIs can describe mistakes that they made on this front, the tensions that they created, and the complicated backtracking that they had to do to make up for their mistakes.

In another example, there is clear consensus that even if an existing lead agency is selected (such as a CDC or a settlement house), it must have a resident base and a record of being an effective and inclusive community planner. One funder reported a positive experience: "Lead organizations, well chosen, have the capacity to go out and bring other people to a table that is created out of their own will, for the good of their own community."

Regardless of the ultimate structure of the initiative, a series of tailored management and technical support activities are implied. For example, a new collaborative is likely to have a whole range of needs from group-building and joint "visioning" exercises to establishing a checking account. The lead agency approach has its own start-up needs:

> **If you're going to go with a lead agency, give them a chance to get their feet on the ground, figure out what direction they think they need to go in. And then build their collaborative, and open up a very democratic process. But [the challenge is to] not put them in the same boat as everybody else in the community because then they're not going to be able to exercise their leadership role.**

Funding and Spending Issues

Three funding issues that are particular to CCIs seem to be emerging: the use of funds, the structure of funds, and the relationship between the funder and the initiative.

The use of funds. Despite their ambitious goals CCIs are not generally wealthy undertakings. Their funding is not of a magnitude to finance new services, new housing, new jobs, new commercial development, and the like. Funds are used instead for staffing the initiative, for community planning, for training and capacity building, for seed money for new projects that will attract and leverage large-scale financing downstream, and for "glue" money to bring activities and institutions together in an effort to produce synergy. The most important characteristic of the funds is that they are flexible.

The structure of funding. Given the long-term nature of the CCI approach and mission, long-term funding is critical to the success of an initiative. (Most participants define long-term as at least ten years.) It not only allows initiatives to develop far-reaching change objectives, but, just as important, it creates a longer window for the initiative to build its support base in the community, develop its governance structure, and put in place an implementation strategy that builds incrementally from short-term activities. The funding must allow time for the laying of a foundation that will support successful implementation and community building. Unfortunately, most funding cycles are of shorter duration than is required to put into place a sustained process of neighborhood transformation. The danger of a short-term funding commitment is that initiatives will be tempted to deliver quickly on "show me" products at the expense of investing in community building.

Long-term funding that appreciates the importance and pace of community building still needs to be strategically structured and to include some form of accountability. One director even feels that a guarantee of long-term funding can encourage initiative participants to get "soft" and can remove the incentive for short-term action. Several participants across groups suggest that foundations should not put all the money up front because a sudden influx of money can distort the planning process: while it may serve to bring a range of actors to the table, it can lead to a focus on distribution of dollars rather than the development of a collaborative process and a shared strategic plan. Several funders and CCI directors suggest that a series of grants for planning, organizational development, capacity-building, and implementation, given out on the basis of mutually agreed-upon evidence of short-term progress, is in the best interest of both parties. In fact, some suggest that it is not even necessary for major funding to flow in the early stages of an initiative, that funding should instead serve as an incentive for action and reward for progress. Thus while the funder needs to commit a significant level of funding in order to be taken seriously, the important element is the commitment of major, long-term support, not necessarily the up-front allocation of those dollars.

The role of the funder. Experience with the inside-outside tension shows that the principal funder of a CCI often plays several roles beyond providing core funding. The funder may frame the initiative conceptually, establish ground rules for action, define initiative goals,

69

GETTING

STARTED:

FINDINGS

FROM

CCI

PRACTICE

identify and convene participants, and define the terms of success. The funder may also serve as an important spokesperson for the initiative over time in the policy world and among other potential funders.

This enhanced role places special demands on a funder's ability to act as a collaborative partner in the initiative and to navigate the line between providing helpful guidance, direction, and accountability on the one hand and imposing its authority from the outside on the other. Thus, amid all of the many groundbreaking activities that a CCI must do, it must also develop new terms for the relationship between the initiative and the funder, one that is a working partnership where both sides can grow, change, and continue to support each another as the initiative develops.

Staffing and Technical Assistance

CCI participants across the board agree that staffing the initiative is decisively important, but that its importance is often underestimated. Strategic choices regarding staffing appear to be critical for the operational success of CCIs for two principal reasons.

The first is that, because CCIs are underspecified at their outset, it falls upon the staff to develop as well as to manage the initiative—as one person described it, "to invent the plane while you fly it." Thus, the flexibility that characterizes so many dimensions of CCIs heightens the importance of the staff role. Moreover, the role of the staff person is likely to change over the course of the initiative, and the visioning talents needed to set the direction for the initiative are not the same as the practical skills required for day-to-day implementation.

Second, because of the breadth of the goals of CCIs and the range of participants involved, initiative staff are asked to mediate between a number of constituencies. Consequently, they require strong organizational and communication skills, political acumen, and an ability to work across a number of substantive areas at once. All participants agree that it is less important to find someone who is technically sophisticated (since technical assistance on particular issues can be contracted for) or who is already familiar with the neighborhood than to recruit someone with strong leadership and process skills.

There does not appear to be any natural "pipeline" for CCI staff development, and sponsors have encountered difficulty locating a pool of candidates. Moreover, given the range of duties they fulfill, staff "burn-out" is, not surprisingly, a significant problem. The process of putting resources in place to support staff in their work needs to be thought through more systematically.

Participants also agree that the provision of technical assistance of all forms—from help on process issues such as board development and strategic planning to consultation around technical issues such as housing development and project-related investments—is critical to the success of a CCI. But TA provision is complicated by inside-outside tensions. CCI directors, staff and governance members argue for greater control over the selection and direction of technical assistance providers as a way of ensuring a good match between provider and neighborhood needs and of holding the technical assistance providers accountable to the local group. In this case, the sponsor might structure the general technical assistance strategy and recommend providers to the initiative, but would not be the final decision-maker. Many also recommend that funds for technical assistance be set aside by the sponsor so that they do not appear to compete with project funds.

The following are suggested ways to ensure that technical assistance is used to best advantage:

- An initiative must be clear about its definition of the problem and what is needed, so it can use technical assistance effectively and not be driven by it.

- It is critical to engage technical assistance providers who know how to listen to the initiative and community, provide practical options to accomplish what needs to get done, and then allow the initiative to decide next steps.

- Technical assistance need not come from professionals or academics; at times, peer-to-peer consulting or input from neighborhood people can be the best assistance, especially in areas such as community organizing or recruiting and engaging residents.

- Community control of technical assistance funding and contracts can help make sure the initiative gets what it wants.

By and large, initiatives report more success with "technical" technical assistance (on issues such as housing development or school reform) than with "process" technical assistance (on topics such as strategic planning, management, or community engagement). Given the complexity of the task at hand, initiatives may be served by designating a "coach" for the initiative: an objective party who can provide advice, support, guidance, and encouragement to the various players in the initiative. One of the primary roles of the coach would be to help the other players in the initiative to recognize and work through the

71

GETTING

STARTED:

FINDINGS

FROM

CCI

PRACTICE

fundamental tensions that must be negotiated as the initiative develops. This role could be played by an individual or institution. One emerging mechanism for managing this process is the locally based intermediary. Politically independent, in part because it does not compete for funding with local agencies, and able to work at various levels, the intermediary can convene diverse stakeholders to discuss options for change, help to staff the change process, and build local capacity for reform, often using data and research as organizing tools.

Evaluation

Evaluation of CCIs is far more complicated than evaluation of more circumscribed programs. Because of this complexity, and because of the experimental nature of CCIs, many funders have invested heavily in the evaluation of CCIs. They aim both to maximize the learning that comes out of the initiatives and to advance methodology in the evaluation field. Important lessons are being learned by CCI evaluators, funders, and initiatives, at this point having more to do with specifying the nature of the problem of evaluating CCIs than with devising solutions to those problems. But general guidance can be derived from recent experience.

From a research perspective, CCI evaluations are problematic for several reasons. First, the initiatives have multiple, broad goals, the achievement of which depends on an ongoing process of interaction or "synergistic" change. Capturing change at all levels and across all sectors is a key challenge, as is determining how to measure the degree to which an initiative is exploiting interdependencies. Second, the particular objectives identified and strategies chosen to promote progress toward these goals often develop and change over time. CCIs are learning enterprises and develop organically as they go along. Third, many of the activities and their intended outcomes are difficult to measure. Developing a way to assess such concepts as capacity building, social capital, and leadership development will be crucial to making judgments about CCI effectiveness. Finally, the units of action for these efforts—neighborhoods—are complex, open systems in which it is virtually impossible to disentangle all of the many variables that may influence both the conduct and outcomes of initiatives. Evaluators, therefore, face tremendous difficulty in drawing causal links between initiative-sponsored actions and community-level outcomes.

One activity that appears to characterize the task of the CCI evaluator is to assist the various initiative stakeholders to gain clarity on the overall vision or "theory of change" of the effort; that is, on long-term outcomes and the strategies that are intended to produce them. The evaluator's inquiry skills and methodological expertise can then help an otherwise underspecified initiative to identify the interim outcomes or markers of progress that correspond, at least theoretically, to those longer term outcomes. Once those steps occur, a review of measures and methods for obtaining those measures can be undertaken by the evaluator in collaboration with the community and the funder.

These activities clearly depart from the evaluator's traditional role and place evaluators in the midst of process-product and inside-outside tensions. For example, evaluators often find themselves playing a quasi-technical assistance role that includes strategic planning, information referral, project reporting, and public relations.

To make the most effective use of resources and serve the interests of the initiative, evaluators are likely to adapt the evaluation methodology over the course of the initiative to match the pace of progress. In the early years, when the CCI is focusing on planning, building relationships, and developing capacity, documentation and ongoing feedback to aid course correction may be most appropriate. The evaluator may work intensively at this time to help identify the initiative's theory of change, and baseline data may also be collected, with the understanding that changes in major social indicators are only likely occur over the long run. Then, later in the initiative, as strategic plans are completed and projects are put in place, a more rigorous, outcome-oriented evaluation may be appropriate. This strategy suggests that a range of methodologies and both quantitative and qualitative data will need to be woven together. Finally, most initiative participants stress the importance of developing an internal capacity for self-monitoring and assessment, and suggest that this should become a core element in any evaluation plan.

Developing Programmatic Strategies

Although CCIs have a comprehensive mandate, it is important to get started *somewhere* and not feel compelled to start with a fully fleshed-out implementation plan. A short-term focus at the beginning helps to avoid getting "stuck" in discussions about the broad long-term vision at the expense of action. The challenge is to maintain the balance between attention to short- and long-term objectives.

73

GETTING

STARTED:

FINDINGS

FROM

CCI

PRACTICE

There is general agreement that there is no one right place for a CCI to start. The choice should be made based on the neighborhood context and the particular goals of the initiative planners. The starting point can be at the individual, neighborhood, or systems level or in any domain of importance to the neighborhood. Participants suggest that some combination of the following criteria constitute the most effective way to identify a starting point:

- build on existing assets

- respond to community needs

- mobilize broad participation

- target short-term, visible accomplishments

- aim to leverage changes in other areas

One approach that has gained popularity among initiatives is to build on individual and neighborhood "assets." In the past, strategies at the individual level have focused on reducing or eliminating deficits or problems that present barriers to change. For example, illiteracy and lack of marketable skills, poor work habits, substance abuse and health problems, and family violence have all been the subject of numerous, usually categorical, change efforts. Similarly, community needs assessments have focused on defining and prioritizing the problems facing the neighborhood. More recently, there has been a movement to identify resident and neighborhood assets and to design the CCI strategy to build on them. This does not imply that more traditional service strategies are excluded, only that taking advantage of strengths confers important additional strategic benefits. Several participants speak, for example, to the important role that racial pride and cultural tradition can play in community development. Moreover, since an asset-based approach identifies neighborhood leadership, it can provide guidance in involving those leaders in the early development of the initiative.

Perhaps the most important element of a comprehensive approach—even more important than the choice of a starting point— is the capacity to establish links across projects, to build gradually from a focus on the chosen starting point to a broad range of work. The notion is that specific, necessarily limited, change activities must "catalyze" action in other areas, create "synergy" across actions, and lead to a whole that is greater than the sum of the parts. Given limited resources, every action must serve a number of functions if change of significant scope and scale is to occur. Some participants talked about creating a "snowball effect" or building a "momentum for change." One evaluator described this process as follows:

> **An initiative is successful not because the people get together and make comprehensive change, but because the changes they make and the process that is entailed somehow provoke an across-the-board response, so that the police start doing their job, and the fire department starts coming to the fires, and the streets start to get paved, and the services start to get delivered, and the schools start to get better.... If you're solely reliant on what the initiative does alone, then you never realize the vision.**

It is critical for CCIs to be strategic about their choices regarding deployment of staff and resources. Therefore, the most strategic point of entry is one from which a progressively more comprehensive and synergistic approach can best be developed.

Small successes at the neighborhood level can serve to help the initiative gain momentum and give those already involved a sense of accomplishment. Several participants gave examples of short-term accomplishments in their initiatives that have served to mobilize support: getting drug dealers out of a park, preventing a school from being built next to a prison, closing a bar, and putting in a four-way stop sign. They note that the key to using these accomplishments to maximum advantage is to make sure that they are part of a larger plan that links the specific action to the broader vision and that identifies related areas of activity that could be catalyzed by early successes in the initial area. Articulating and working to exploit these linkages among areas helps to reduce the danger of discrete activities becoming ends in themselves and diverting energy and resources away from implementation of the initiative's comprehensive agenda. This approach requires an entrepreneurial and opportunistic stance, with a keen eye to the catalytic potential of a single activity to contribute to the initiative's longer term objectives.

Appendix A

Roundtable Members
May 1997

Harold Richman (Co-Chair)
    Director
    Chapin Hall Center for Children
    The University of Chicago

Lisbeth B. Schorr (Co-Chair)
    Lecturer in Social Medicine
    Director, Project on Effective Services
    Harvard University

Michael Bailin
    President
    Edna McConnell Clark Foundation

Douglas Besharov
    Resident Scholar
    American Enterprise Institute
    for Public Policy Research

Angela G. Blackwell
    Senior Vice President
    The Rockefeller Foundation

Barbara B. Blum
    Senior Fellow
    National Center for Children
    in Poverty
    Columbia University

Geoffrey Canada
    Executive Director
    Rheedlen Centers for Families
    and Children

Peter Edelman
    Professor of Law
    Georgetown University Law Center

John W. Gardner
    Professor
    Stanford University

Sid Gardner
    Director
    Center for Collaboration for Children

Stephen Goldsmith
    Mayor
    City of Indianapolis

Patricia Graham
    President
    The Spencer Foundation

Ralph Hamilton
    Director of Florida Philanthropy
    The John D. and Catherine T.
    MacArthur Foundation

Ruby P. Hearn
    Senior Vice President
    The Robert Wood Johnson
    Foundation

David Hornbeck
    Superintendent
    School District of Philadelphia

Craig Howard
    Program Officer
    James Irvine Foundation

Otis S. Johnson
    Executive Director
    Chatham-Savannah
    Youth Futures Authority

Anne C. Kubisch
  Director
  The Aspen Institute Roundtable on
  Comprehensive Community
  Initiatives

Jack Litzenberg
  Poverty Team Coordinator
  The Charles Stewart
  Mott Foundation

Susan Lloyd
  Senior Program Officer
  The John D. and Catherine T.
  MacArthur Foundation

Jack Mawdsley
  Vice President for Youth
  W. K. Kellogg Foundation

Anita Miller
  Program Director
  Comprehensive Community
  Revitalization Program

Janice Molnar
  Deputy Director
  Human Development and
  Reproductive Health
  The Ford Foundation

William A. Morrill
  President
  Mathtech, Inc.

Douglas W. Nelson
  President
  The Annie E. Casey Foundation

Terry Peterson
  Counselor to the Secretary
  U.S. Department of Education

Ron Register
  Executive Director
  Cleveland Community Building
  Initiative

Julius B. Richmond
  Department of Social Medicine
  Harvard University

Michael Stegman
  Assistant Secretary
  Policy Development and Research
  U.S. Department of Housing and
  Urban Development

Gary Walker
  President
  Public/Private Ventures

Appendix B

Focus Group Participants
by Peer Group

Evaluators

Susan Beekman
General Accounting Office
Washington, DC

Prudence Brown
Chapin Hall Center for Children
Chicago, IL

Robert Chaskin
Chapin Hall Center for Children
Chicago, IL

Michael Giles
Emory University
Atlanta, GA

Judith England Joseph
General Accounting Office
Washington, DC

Gary Miller
Change, Inc.
Minneapolis, MN

Dennis Rose
Dennis Rose and Associates
Davis, CA

Joseph Stillman
The Conservation Company
New York, NY

Mercer Sullivan
Vera Institute of Justice
New York, NY

Avis Vidal
New School for Social Research
New York, NY

Funders

Michael Bangser
Hartford Foundation for Giving
Hartford, CT

Carole Berde
McKnight Foundation
Minneapolis, MN

Carol Glazer
Local Initiatives Support Corporation
New York, NY

Ralph Hamilton
The John D. and Catherine T.
MacArthur Foundation
Palm Beach Gardens, FL

Kathryn Merchant
Neighborhood Preservation Initiative
New Haven, CT

Mariam Noland
Community Foundation for
Southeastern Michigan
Detroit, MI

Anne Romasco
James C. Penney Foundation
New York, NY

Roundtable Members

Angela Blackwell
   The Rockefeller Foundation
   New York, NY

Barbara Blum
   Foundation for Child Development
   New York, NY

Robert Curvin
   The Ford Foundation
   New York, NY

Peter Edelman
   U.S. Department of Health and
   Human Services
   Washington, DC

Sid Gardner
   Center for Collaboration for Children
   Fullerton, CA

Craig Howard
   The James Irvine Foundation
   San Francisco, CA

Otis Johnson
   Chatham-Savannah Youth Futures
   Authority

Rebecca Riley
   The John D. and Catherine T.
   MacArthur Foundation
   Chicago, IL

James Rouse
   Enterprise Foundation
   Columbia, MD

Lisbeth Schorr
   Harvard Project on Effective Services
   Washington, DC

Ralph Smith
   The Annie E. Casey Foundation
   Baltimore, MD

Observers

Eric Brettschneider
   Agenda for Children Tomorrow
   New York, NY

Maria Casey
   Urban Strategies Council
   Oakland, CA

James Gibson
   Urban Institute
   Washington, DC

Andrew Mott
   Center for Community Change
   Washington, DC

Arthur Naparstak
   Case Western Reserve University
   Cleveland, OH

Michael Rubinger
   Fund for Urban Neighborhood
   Development
   Philadelphia, PA
   Savannah, GA

Thomas Seessell
   SEEDCO
   New York, NY

Mitchell Sviridoff
   Independent Consultant
   Gay Head, MA

Directors/Staff

Veronica Barela
   NEWSED Community Development
   Corporation
   Denver, CO

Don Blake
   Upper Albany Neighborhood
   Collaborative
   Hartford, CT

Harold Cordier
   Iron Triangle Community
   Collaborative
   Richmond, CA

Patrick Costigan
   Community Building in Partnership
   Program
   Baltimore, MD

Margaret DeSantis
Warren Conner Development
Coalition
Detroit, MI

Sarah Ford
Milwaukee Foundation
Milwaukee, WI

Janice Foster
Community Foundation of Greater
Memphis
Memphis, TN

Pete Garcia
Chicanos Por La Causa
Phoenix, AZ

Roberto Garcia
The Cantera Project
Hato Rey, PR

Martin Gerry
The Austin Project
Austin, TX

Edward Hayes
The Community Foundation of
Greater Memphis
Memphis, TN

Betty Herrera
The Piton Foundation
Denver, CO

Pearl Howell
East Bay Funders
Oakland, CA

Robin Hynicka
Frankford Group Ministry
Philadelphia, PA

Leonard Jackson
Community Building in Partnership
Baltimore, MD

Patricia Jenny
New York Community Trust
New York, NY

Sandra Knox
Neighborhood Housing Services, Inc.
Pasadena, CA

Craig Lewis
Austin Labor Force Intermediary
Chicago, IL

William Linder
New Community Corporation
Newark, NJ

Cheryl Lockhart
Community Building in Partnership
Baltimore, MD

May Louie
Dudley Street Neighborhood
Initiative
Roxbury, MA

Albert Lovata
Dudley Street Neighborhood
Initiative
Roxbury, MA

Anita Miller
Comprehensive Community
Revitalization Program
New York, NY

Gus Newport
Partnership for Neighborhood
Initiatives
Boyton Beach, FL

Shem Shakir
Frogtown Action Alliance
St. Paul, MN

Carey Shea
Local Initiative Support Corporation
New York, NY

Jane Smith
The Atlanta Project
Atlanta, GA

Joanne Stately
Children, Families and Community
Initiative
St. Paul, MN

Barbara Washington
Community Foundation for
Southeastern Michigan
Detroit, MI

Autrie Moore Williams
Glades Community Development
Corporation
Belle Glade, FL

Neighborhood Residents*

Josie Acosta
NEWSED Community Development
Corporation*
Denver, CO

Antionnette Andino
The Milwaukee Foundation*
Milwaukee, WI

Frances Barnes
The Community Foundation of
Greater Memphis*
Memphis, TN

Jackie DeWitt
The Atlanta Project*
Atlanta, GA

Dwight Fischer
East Bay Funders*
Oakland, CA

Diane Franklin
Pasadena Neighborhood Housing
Services*
Pasadena, CA

Carl Hardrick
Upper Albany Neighborhood
Collaborative*
Albany, NY

Kate Lane
Bethel New Life*
Chicago, IL

Pauline Lockett
Glades Community Development
Corporation*
Belle Glade, FL

Elisabethe Mack
Community Foundation for
Southeastern Michigan*
Detroit, MI

Nelson Parrish
The Pew Charitable Trusts*
Philadelphia, PA

Rudy Perez
Chicanos por La Causa*
Phoenix, AZ

J. Allen Stokes
The Milwaukee Foundation*
Milwaukee, WI

Clarence Winston
Cleveland Community Building
Initiative*
Cleveland, OH

Members of Governance Structures*

Brenda Bell Brown
Children, Families and Community
Initiative*
St. Paul, MN

Connie De Lury
The Pew Charitable Trusts*
Philadelphia, PA

Prentice Deadrick
Pasadena Neighborhood Housing
Services*
Pasadena, CA

Jeannette Dexter
Glades Community Development
Corporation*
Belle Glade, FL

Ruth Dyson
Marshall Heights Community
Development Organization*
Washington, DC

F. Nur Jawad
Milwaukee Foundation*
Milwaukee, WI

Vincent Kountz
Community Foundation for
Southeastern Michigan*
Detroit, MI

Kaye Lawler
  The Community Foundation
  of Greater Memphis*
  Memphis, TN

Lolita McDavid
  Cleveland Community Building
  Initiative*
  Cleveland, OH

John Mejia
  East Bay Funders*
  San Francisco, CA

James Milner
  The Atlanta Project*
  Atlanta, GA

Sheila Radford Hill
  Bethel New Life*
  Chicago, IL

Sandra Santa Cruz
  NEWSED Community Development
  Corporation*
  Denver, CO

Lawrence Taylor
  East Bay Funders*
  Oakland, CA

Michael Whalen
  Chicanos por La Causa*
  Phoenix, AZ

*Listed with Nominating Agency

Appendix C

Methodology
and Questions

Sample Selection

For the purposes of this report, a comprehensive community initiative has three defining characteristics:

- It aims to promote positive change in individual, family, and neighborhood circumstances.
- It works to improve physical, economic, and social conditions at the neighborhood level.
- It places strong emphasis on community building and neighborhood empowerment.

Working from this definition, the project team reviewed reports and consulted experts in the field to devise a list of comprehensive community initiatives from which to invite representatives for the peer group sessions. The team in no way pretends that the group of initiatives that eventually participated is exhaustive. Given the fluid parameters of the CCI definition, it inevitably represents only a sample of these efforts. Moreover, while some of the initiatives that were included may already be working on all the above-stated goals, others may be evolving in that direction.

The project team believes that they are nonetheless illustrative of the field and that conclusions based on their experiences can speak legitimately for the field as a whole.

In the end, eighteen CCIs were represented. In addition, four other community development corporations (CDCs) were invited to participate in the process because they generally conform to the criteria the team put forth for CCI designation and because of their rich history and experience. (See Appendix D for full list of participating initiatives.)

Process

The project team scheduled eleven one-day peer-group sessions over the course of a two-month period, May 22–July 19, 1995. The peer groups are listed with the number of sessions held:

- funders (1 session)
- directors (2 sessions)
- governance structure participants, such as board or collaborative members (2 sessions)
- evaluators (1 session)
- staff members (1 session)

- residents of communities where initiatives are underway (2 sessions)
- observers of the field, such as policy makers, technical assistance providers, and academicians (1 session)
- Roundtable members (1 session)

The project team identified all peer group participants except residents and members of governance structures, who were nominated by CCI directors or funders. Directors also nominated some of the staff members who participated. By the end of the process, the insights of 94 actors in the field had been solicited.

At least four members of the seven-member project team were present at any given session. Two members of the team were responsible for facilitating the discussion, and two other members were responsible for distilling the information into preliminary synopses. Team members interchanged roles from session to session. Each session was taped and transcribed, and discussants were granted anonymity to encourage their most forthright responses.

Prior to their attendance at the meeting, discussants were provided with a detailed list of written questions upon which to reflect. The questions, listed below, covered seven core issues:

- comprehensiveness of program
- community building
- decision-making and governance
- contextual dimensions that affect the unfolding of the CCI
- financial, technical, and institutional support

- interim markers of progress and ultimate outcomes
- evaluation

Although questions were tailored to each peer group classification, the essence of the questions remained the same across groups. However, midway through the process, questions were reorganized to allow the theme of community building, which had emerged as a central issue in early sessions, to be discussed more thoroughly in subsequent sessions.

Transcriptions of the sessions, which were based on responses to the seven core categories outlined above, served as the project's "raw data." The raw data were reviewed in conjunction with selective initiative documents and the team's preliminary synopses. After a review of the material in its totality, the team reorganized the data into the format presented in this report.

Discussants were asked to speak from personal experiences. Because of the nature of CCIs, some of the discussants were actually speaking from experience in multiple roles. Moreover, a few of the participants had experience from more than one initiative and spoke from the perspective of the same role in multiple initiatives. This overlap in roles and initiative perspective added to the richness of the discussions.

Sample Questions

1. Comprehensiveness

The purpose of this session is to explore lessons learned about the pros and cons of a comprehensive approach—as opposed to focusing on specific sectors or problem areas—and to explore the utility/feasibility of the concept of "synergy."

Questions to provoke your thinking:

• Based on your experience, what conclusions/lessons would you draw about the best starting place for a community initiative? For example, what difference do you think it would make if an initiative started out focusing on social services and then moved into economic development or vice versa? Is there a particular sequencing of program components that works better than others?

• How much emphasis should CCIs place on trying to achieve "comprehensiveness"? In what ways has the concept facilitated various initiatives' efforts and in what ways has it hampered them?

• Do you have any evidence that there is synergy among various elements of a comprehensive initiative, and, if so, how would you characterize it? What strategies have people used to achieve it?

• Under which circumstances—for example, level of community resources, type of outside support, and so on—would you say that notions of comprehensiveness and synergy are most useful? When are they not?

• Other general lessons about comprehensiveness?

2. Governance

The purpose of this session is to explore lessons learned about the forms and structures of governance that work best to promote various governance objectives.

Questions to provoke your thinking:

• What attributes of the governance structure of community initiatives work best to promote (or inhibit):

• community participation in the planning, management, and implementation of the initiative

• collaboration among institutions and organizations

• efficient and effective decision-making

• getting the work done

• legitimacy within and beyond the community

• accountability

• What are the effects, both positive and negative, of engaging community members in the governance of an initiative on its implementation, impact, legitimacy, and sustainability?

• Based on your experience, do you think that different types of governance structures might work better during different phases of an initiative, and, if so, how best to engineer the evolution of a governance structure?

- Based on your experience, what would you see as the tradeoffs associated with creating a new structure (for example, a neighborhood collaborative) for carrying out the work of the CCI as opposed to working through an existing "lead" organization?

- How would your recommendations about types of governance structures vary according to the level of social organization in a community, the capacity of existing community institutions, and so on?

- Other general lessons about governance?

3. Leadership Development and Community Building

The purpose of this session is to explore lessons learned about strategies for building "community" and developing local capacity for community improvement.

Questions to provoke your thinking:

- Which strategies followed by community initiatives have been most effective for developing individual, organizational, and community-level capacity for identifying and implementing solutions to local problems?

- In your experience, is there generally agreement among all the participants in an initiative about the community building (or empowerment) aspects of the initiative-its definition, its importance, the strategies for achieving it?

- Based on your experience, do you think that community building should be an end in and of itself, or should it be viewed as an instrument for achieving social and economic outcomes?

- Based on your experience, what lessons can you draw about how program strategies and objectives should differ given different pre-existing levels of social organization and types of community leadership? How should they evolve over time?

- How do other neighborhood dynamics, such as race and class, influence the community building agenda, either positively or negatively?

- Other general lessons about community building?

4. Context

The purpose of this session is to explore the contextual factors that facilitate or hinder comprehensive community initiatives and the extent to which CCIs can have an impact on the larger system.

Questions to provoke your thinking:

- What kinds of support from local and state government have been most important to CCIs? What aspects of the public sector's operations have been most harmful?

- How well do the CCIs interact with other ongoing initiatives in particular neighborhoods?

- Based on your experience, are there certain macroeconomic or political contextual factors which must be in place for an initiative to thrive? Are there certain contexts in which a CCI should not be attempted?

• In what ways are the policy changes in Washington likely to affect the current generation of CCIs, positively or negatively, and what changes might you recommend that they adopt in response?

• Based on your experience, how much should systems reform be an objective of CCIs?

• How do the following characteristics of a neighborhood affect the unfolding of an initiative:

  • existence of physical, organizational, human or capital resources
  • size of neighborhood
  • physical characteristics
  • ethnic, racial, cultural dynamics
  • degree of cohesion, neighborhood identification, and social capital
  • connection to larger social, economic and political community

• Other general lessons about context?

5. Financial and Technical Support

The purpose of this session is to attempt to distill lessons about the kinds of technical, human, and financial resources that are most important for CCI success.

Questions to provoke your thinking:

• Are CCIs generally funded at the correct level? What does the funding "buy," and is it allocated appropriately? What recommendation would you make to funders of future initiatives about level of funding, flexibility of funding, duration of funding, purpose for which funds can

be used, and review/accountability procedures?

• Based on your experience, what roles, beyond providing financial support, are most helpful/harmful for a funder to play?

• What are the ways in which technical assistance on "process" issues-such as outreach, leadership development, planning-have been most helpful to CCIs? In what ways has it been harmful?

• What are the ways in which technical assistance on substantive issues-such as development financing, child development, neighborhood safety-have been most helpful to CCIs? In what ways has it been harmful?

• What lessons have you learned about staffing CCIs with respect to types of training, interpersonal skills, level of professionalism, knowledge of the community, cultural issues? What are the critical functions of the initiative staff?

• What kinds of technical support have greatly aided CCIs, such as MIS or other data-based activities, participation in cross-site discussions, and so on?

• Other general lessons about outside support?

6. Evaluation and Outcomes

The purpose of this session is to explore those aspects of the evaluation process that have been most helpful and most problematic and to distill any lessons about markers of progress.

Questions to provoke your thinking:

- What aspects of current evaluation strategies are most helpful in terms of:
  - managing the initiative
  - assessing progress toward outcomes
  - reporting to funders and the outside world
  - community building
- In what ways does evaluation cause problems?
- Who sets the outcomes for which initiatives are held accountable?
- What are appropriate long-term outcomes to seek in terms of impact on individuals and families, community change, organizational change, system change?
- What shorter term indicators of progress are most useful? Which are most easily measured?
- Are there "negative" markers, that is, markers that indicate that the initiative is not working?
- Other general lessons about outcomes?

7. General Reflections

- Is the current generation of community initiatives significantly different from those of the past (for example, community development corporations)? How and in what ways? What lessons have they learned and what have they missed?
- If the director of a new initiative asked you for the most important lesson you have learned about comprehensive community initiatives, what would you say?

- What do you anticipate will be the most difficult challenges facing CCIs during the next year? The next five years?

Appendix D

Sources of
Additional Information

Most of the organizations represented in the focus groups are listed below with contact information for readers who wish additional information about the initiatives themselves.

Also, the National Community Building Network, the national association of CCIs, is sponsoring a project based at the Urban Institute to create a data base on CCIs. For further information on the data base, contact:

Maria-Rosario Jackson
  The Urban Institute
  2100 M Street, NW
  Washington, DC 20037
  Phone: (202) 857-8689
  Fax: (202) 659-8985
  E-mail: mjackson@UI.urban.org

AGENDA FOR CHILDREN TOMORROW (ACT)

Eric Brettschneider
  80 LaFayette Street
  Room 1425 A
  New York, NY 10013
  Phone: (212) 266-3392
  Fax: (212) 266-3227

THE AUSTIN INITIATIVE

Craig J. Lewis
  Chief Executive Officer
  Shorebank Neighborhood Institute
  5420 West Roosevelt Road
  Chicago, IL 60644
  Phone: (773) 854-4360
  Fax: (773) 854-4380

COMMUNITY BUILDING INITIATIVE

Mathew Wexler
  Program Officer in Research
  Development
  Local Initiative Support Corporation
  733 Third Avenue
  New York, NY 10017
  Phone: (212) 455-9800
  Fax: (212) 682-5929

COMMUNITY BUILDING IN PARTNERSHIP

Doug Stanton
Development and Communications
Manager
1137 North Gilmore Street
Baltimore, MD 21217
Phone: (410) 728-8607
Fax: (410) 728-8609

CLEVELAND COMMUNITY BUILDING INITIATIVE

Ronald Register
Executive Director
5000 Euclid Avenue, Suite 200
Cleveland, OH 44103
Phone: (216) 361-9800
Fax: (216) 361-4429

COMPREHENSIVE COMMUNITY REVITALIZATION PROGRAM

Anita Miller
CCRP Program Director
330 Madison Avenue, 30th Floor
New York, NY 10017
Phone: (212) 557-2929
Fax: (212) 557-0003
E-mail: ccrp@igc.org

CHILDREN, FAMILIES AND COMMUNITY INITIATIVES

Valerie Lee
Director
633 University Avenue
St. Paul, MN 55104
Phone: (612) 291-1702
Fax: (612) 291-0737

DUDLEY STREET NEIGHBORHOOD INITIATIVE

Gregory Watson, Executive Director
or
Ros Everdell, Organizing Director
513 Dudley Street
Roxbury, MA 02119
Phone: (617) 442-9670
Fax: (617) 427-8047

FROGTOWN ACTION ALLIANCE

Shem Shakir
Executive Director
689 North Dale Street
St. Paul, MN 55013
Phone: (612) 224-7184
Fax: (612) 224-7348
E-mail: FUBRC@aol.com

GLADES COMMUNITY DEVELOPMENT CORPORATION

Autrey Williams
Executive Director
425 West Canal Street
Belle Grade, FL 33430
Phone: (561) 992-9500
Fax: (561) 992-9501

NEW COMMUNITY CORPORATION

William Linder
Founder
233 West Market Street
Newark, NJ 07103
Phone: (201) 623-2800
Fax: (201) 623-3612

NEIGHBORHOOD AND FAMILY INITIATIVE

Ruth Roman
Program Officer
Ford Foundation
320 East 43rd Street
New York, NY 10017
Phone: (212) 573-5337
Fax: (212) 297-0969

NEIGHBORHOOD PRESERVATION
INITIATIVE

Marisa H. Sheingate
  Project Administrator
  20 Grand Avenue
  New Haven, CT 06513
  Phone: (203) 777-0259
  Fax: (203) 777-2530

NEIGHBORHOOD STRATEGIES
PROJECT

Patricia Jenny
  New York Community Trust
  2 Park Avenue
  New York, NY 10016-9385

PASADENA NEIGHBORHOOD
HOUSING SERVICES

Sandra Knox
  Executive Director
  456 West Montana Street
  Pasadena, CA 91103
  Phone: (626) 794-7191
  Fax: (626) 794-7246

PARTNERSHIP FOR
NEIGHBORHOOD INITIATIVE

Ralph Hamilton
  Director of Florida Philanthropy
  MacArthur Foundation
  Community Initiative Program
  4400 PGA Boulevard
  Admiralty Building #2, Suite 900
  Palm Beach Gardens, FL 33410
  Phone: (561) 626-4800
  Fax: (561) 624-4948

PROYECTO PENINSULA DE
CANTERA

Roberto Garcia Rodriguez
  Executive Director
  Avenida Barbaso 618
  Hato Rey, Puerto Rico 00917

REBUILDING COMMUNITIES
INITIATIVE

Garland A. Yates
  Senior Associate
  The Annie E. Casey Foundation
  701 St. Paul Street
  Baltimore, MD 21202

THE ATLANTA PROJECT (TAP)

The America Project
  The Carter Collaboration Center
  675 Ponce de Leon Avenue, NE
  Post Office Box 5317
  Atlanta, GA 30307-5317
  Phone: (404) 881-3400
  Fax: (404) 881-3482
  http://www.emory.edu/Carter_Center/